What Do You Need Today?

HOPE LYDA

HARVEST HOUSE PUBLISHERS
EUGENE, OREGON

*I am grateful to Harvest House for partnering with me on this book.
Thank you to those who were my generous readers in the process—
Dawn Cadwell, Carolyn McCready, Ruth Samsel, Kimberly Shumate,
and special thanks to LaRae Weikert for her life-coach perspective.*

Unless otherwise indicated, all Scripture quotations are taken from the Holy Bible,
New International Version®, NIV®. Copyright © 1973, 1978, 1984, 2011 by Biblica, Inc.®
Used by permission. All rights reserved worldwide.

Verses marked ESV are taken from The ESV® Bible (The Holy Bible, English Standard Version®),
copyright © 2001 by Crossway, a publishing ministry of Good News Publishers. Used by permission.
All rights reserved.

Verses marked NLT are taken from the Holy Bible, New Living Translation, copyright © 1996, 2004,
2015 by Tyndale House Foundation. Used by permission of Tyndale House Publishers, Inc., Carol
Stream, Illinois 60188. All rights reserved.

Verses marked NKJV are taken from the New King James Version®. Copyright © 1982 by Thomas
Nelson, Inc. Used by permission. All rights reserved.

Cover and interior design by Studio Gearbox
Cover photo © Allexxandar, Alexander_Evgenyevich / Shutterstock

Ⓗ is a federally registered trademark of the Hawkins Children's LLC. Harvest House Publishers, Inc.,
is the exclusive licensee of the trademark.

What Do You Need Today?

Printed in the United States of America

21 22 23 24 25 26 27 28 29 / VP / 10 9 8 7 6 5 4 3 2 1

Contents

WHAT DO YOU NEED *today?*

We aren't often asked this question. And we rarely ask this question of ourselves. So take a moment before you follow the impulse to move things along quickly by saying, "Oh, nothing. I'm good. I'm fine."

I'll repeat it. Slowly. Kindly. Invitingly. Sincerely.

What do you need today?

Hold the question up to the light. Cradle it like a gift. Present it to your heart, spirit, and mind and see which part of you longs to answer.

When is the last time someone asked you this and waited to hear the answer? If you are unsure how to respond, you're not alone. I believe we aren't able to access the answer immediately because we become distanced from our heart needs by busyness, worries, demands at work and home, guilt, years of suppressing what our needs are, or years of feeling overlooked.

For the sake of time or energy, we put aside our needs to

deal with what immediately requires attention, and then we forget to return to the tender work of exploring what our spirits seek for refreshment, hope, and joy. God welcomes you to intimately know the landscape of your heart and to enter this place of sanctuary with him.

Your answer matters. Your need might be for peace and quiet while you take a bath. Or maybe you desire direction in your vocation. Or a sense of restoration. Every one of the heart needs is important.

I'm here to help you tap into those needs. I'll be right beside you throughout this journey. I want to hold this space as you discover how it feels to have your needs heard and received by a gentle listener who responds with empathy, openness, and humor. Thanks for including me. Okay, I invited myself along . . . but I have the best of intentions. In life, when I'm not here with you, I am a writing companion and coach for authors, a caregiver, a spiritual director, and an author of books of prayer, comfort, and life and faith exploration. I come alongside you to offer encouragement that is born of a prayerful spirit.

For this journey, think of me as a spiritual and life concierge who is at your beck and call. Ring the bell. Buzz the buzzer.

Snap your fingers. Yell "yoo hoo" like a longtime neighbor. Or wave me over. I'm ready to sit with you and . . .

> hold the questions and answers with hope
> help untangle strands of hard words or struggles
> be in silence until discomfort becomes ease
> wait with patience for buried needs to surface
> laugh about the awkward times and
> > silly moments
> pray with you and for you
> drape a blanket across your shoulders
> offer "care packages" for each need
> deliver gifts to your heart
> notice God's presence
> encourage your next steps
> celebrate the gift of today with you

After needs repeatedly get buried beneath the demands and distractions, we lose touch with who we are and the value of our days, our lives. I wonder what brings you to self-care. What signaled your soul that it's time to listen within, witness your longings, or cry, laugh, or rant? A personal transition, a worldwide pandemic, or anything in between can be what illuminates a vital truth—to recognize your simplest need is to recognize your deepest need for the Creator.

When you draw from the mercy of God's presence, you partake in the "sacrament of the present moment"—a sentiment from the seventh-century Jesuit priest Jean-Pierre de Caussade, who wrote:

> O, all you who thirst, learn that you have not far to go to find the fountain of living waters; it flows quite close to you in the present moment; therefore hasten to find it. Why, with the fountain so near, do you tire yourselves with running about after every little rill?[1]

Why *do* we tire ourselves? Grab your journal to gather insights and comforts, and let's head to the abundant fountain of living waters for refreshment in this moment.

---

1 Jean-Pierre de Caussade, *Abandonment to Divine Providence* (Northport, AL: Regimen Books, 2018), 49.

To recognize
your simplest need
is to recognize
your deepest need
for the Creator.

I NEED...
a fresh start

It's the perfect day for a new beginning. Clear the way, sweep aside hesitations, and set your sights on the hope of something compelling and brilliant. No need to look back and keep checking to see if a few bad days or moments or even years are trailing behind you like a clumsy detective. You can shake the past and place your purpose and intention in the hands of the one who will make a way for you. God is eager to whisper words of hope to your spirit. He's been preparing your way and awaiting this moment for a long time.

Say goodbye to anything that won't serve you in the days to come. You might be surprised how hard it is to break up with a bad habit, a nickname you always hated as a kid, or a burden you've carried so long that it rests naturally on your hip. (You started to assume it was supposed to be there. It's not. Give it over to God—he is made to carry this weight.) If parting ways with a worry is tough, promise to write it a letter from a better viewpoint up ahead. You can even sign it "xo" if that makes you feel better.

You've cleared what lies behind, now what might hinder your way ahead? Maybe it is a what or a who. Maybe it is you? Don't worry. A lot of us stand in our own way. We can make this all better. Just kindly ask yourself (your old self, your stubborn self, or your slow-to-want-to-change self) to take a bow for all the hard work that paved the way. Then offer yourself a nice comfy seat off to the side of the path where you can rest and be thankful for all the grace that has brought you this far. It'd be quite thoughtful to offer yourself a snack.

There. Now you are safely out of your way. Tended to with loving gestures and satisfying and distracting treats. The you that is moving forward can do so without interference. Oh . . . is there still a what in the way? Name it. Take a close look at it. Maybe it isn't as scary or annoying as you had thought. In fact, maybe it has inspired one of the gifts that will serve you well, like courage or wisdom.

Take a moment to celebrate. This is your reset moment. Sure, it took a few adjustments and goodbyes to get here. But this place of belief and freedom and hope is an amazing spot to stand on. You'll recall it fondly. Do you want to give a speech to mark this occasion? It's an important one. It seems right to me that we bless this fresh start. How about it?

> May the path of your new beginning be
> bathed in assuring light.
> May your companions be mercy and joy.
> And may you treasure a memory from each
> day's adventure with gratitude.

How are you feeling now that you've taken a fresh start step? You are giving your life the fuel of new possibility. Allow it to bolster your morale and boost your energy. When you encounter discouragement, you can revisit this moment. It will be here. And for this journey, I'll be here too. I'll remind you why this choice matters.

This place of
belief and freedom
and hope is an
amazing spot
to stand on.

Care Package

Delivered to Your Heart

Open it. Open it! The package I wish for you: A journal in your favorite color. A bright red reset button to place near you at all times. And a beautiful planner with a red pen so you can mark this as a milestone day. Congrats to you, my friend.

Explorations and Actions

What are your wishes for this beginning?

_____

_____

_____

_____

_____

What has hindered your fresh start in the past? Write a goodbye letter to a worry or difficulty that is in your way. List the tools, people, dreams, and resources you want to bring with you into a new season.

_____

_____

_____

_____

_____

_____

Invite someone to celebrate this fresh start with you. (Who champions you and encourages your journey? Let them in on this happy occasion to make it official.)

_____

_____

_____

_____

God Sees Your Need

This new beginning is a part of the life God is forming through your faithfulness and his.

> *Every house is built by someone,*
> *but God is the builder of everything.*
>
> HEBREWS 3:4

Self-Care Self Talk

I am ready for a reset in this area of my life. I will honor this time by noticing and embracing what invigorates me and feeds my hope.

I NEED...
boldness

Where does our strength of resolve go when the moment comes for us to shine? Why is it that conviction scampers at the first sight of an obstacle? All it takes is a past failure to replay in our minds or the voice of our inner bully saying, *Are you nuts? You can't possibly do this!* and we are looking for an escape, once again.

I know it is tough to evict the negative comments that claim squatters' rights in our brains, especially if people have stated those things at any point in the journey. Healing will come as you turn over those thoughts to God and replace beliefs that cause you to spiral downward with bold truths that lift you spiritually, emotionally upward.

But today . . . today you are ready to speak out or stand up. I see you straighten your posture and look around with wide-open eyes willing to survey what is ahead rather than look away out of fear. I'm certain that good changes are coming. Your step will be so confident and sure that it will make a lasting impression on the path of life. Your release from timidity will empower you to be yourself and prompt others to be themselves.

What will be your act of boldness? Pursuing a new job or a role in a local play? Believing the still, small voice that says you have value or standing strong to create healthy boundaries with unhealthy people? Speaking up for yourself and a need you have or risking neighborhood gossip by painting your living room chartreuse? Whatever it is . . . good for you.

Being bold is not about claiming external power, it is about summoning the strength you know exists within. It is about grabbing the arrows of faith, hope, and uniqueness and aiming and releasing them, one by one, to land smack dab in the center of your purpose. The act of aiming and releasing is the moment of boldness because even if things don't go as planned, a new plan is set in motion. You have changed just by acting with belief. Whatever happens next is fine. In fact, it's fabulous. You will greet the new way with a confident nod and a boisterous "Welcome, courage!"

I wonder, does any of this feel familiar? Do you remember a time when you were bold as a child, youth, or young adult?

I want to hear about the rush of adrenaline as you stepped up with hope or the nervousness as you pressed on despite it. Let your history and journey with God inspire you in your need for boldness today.

What will boldness look like in your life now? When you encounter the situation, the fork in the road, the conversation, or the adversity, you will be empowered by one or all of these:

belief—your motivation

openness—your willingness

love—the state of your heart

daring—a fueled sense of courage

It doesn't have to be a big move to be a bold move. Your courage will be evident in your willingness to listen attentively to someone you don't agree with, volunteer for a task that is in the suburbs of your comfort zone, or greet a new day with faith. Bravo, my friend. You are shedding the restraints of fear. You are replacing self-doubt with God-trust. Embody your new boldness. Notice what looks and feels different as you interact with the world empowered.

It doesn't
have to be a
big move to be
a bold move.

Care Package

Delivered to Your Heart

Some goodies I wish for your bold journey: The recording of a crowd cheering to be played when you need a boost. A vintage silver frame with a photo of you being bold as a kid. And what every ensemble for courage needs—a cape. It's reversible even.

Explorations and Actions

How will you be bold today?

_____

_____

Walk through and write through the elements of BOLD:

Belief—What belief compels you forward?

_____

_____

Openness—Why is now the time to be willing to live with courage?

_____

_____

Love—How are you freed when you view limitless love and not personal power as the source of your strength?

_____

_____

_____

Daring—What will daring look like, feel like in this life situation?

_____

_____

_____

God Sees Your Need

God is with you in this circumstance and has prepared you long before this moment.

> *The spirit God gave us does not make us timid,*
> *but gives us power, love and self-discipline.*
>
> 2 TIMOTHY 1:7

Self-Care Self Talk

My boldness is the strength of God moving in my life. I won't be scared of it; I will be prepared for it.

I NEED...
room to breathe

Sometimes we need a reminder to breathe deeply and intentionally. I'm here because I need it too. Chances are, your body has been asking for room to "just be" for some time. Do you start the day with shallow breathing the moment you awaken because your first thoughts are of how far behind you are? Have you caught yourself drumming your fingers impatiently while waiting for chamomile tea to brew? It's time for some breathing lessons.

The pace of our days rarely lets up and the possibility of finding a time and place to put our feet up sounds impossible. But all you need is waiting for you. There's a wonderful chair near the window you bought for the purpose of sitting (imagine that); and yet, you only sit on it when company comes. There's a circular patch of clover-laced grass beneath an oak tree that beckons a picnic for one. A walking path winds through a dense forest and has plenty of benches along the way for you to rest on and from which you can stare at beauty for refreshment. These gentle spaces exist.

When is the last time you were intentional about carving out time to just be and breathe without telling yourself that you are wasting time? When you think of making room to breathe, what is your first thought? I think about all the worldly pressures I perceive that take up mental space. Soon that sensation of being crowded in my own mind manifests in physical ways. My breathing is shallow. I catch myself yawning big midday because my body is struggling to function with the limited oxygen I'm providing.

How much better it would be for us if we generously provided our bodies what they need to serve us, serve the world, serve God. Finding the cadence of your breath is like the "getting back on a bicycle" scenario. Your body will remember what it feels like to work properly, to propel you toward freedom of movement, and to savor the rush of air. The rhythm God gave you for sustaining life is embedded in the muscle memory of your heart and lungs.

In. Out.

In. Out.

In . . . Out . . .

Just reading these cues will get you started. Pray to find balance. Ask for the peace that surpasses all understanding to reunite your heart, soul, and mind as you breathe in gratitude and breathe out stress. Do this once a day. Soon you'll look forward to releasing your tight shoulders and your wound-up fears during these moments of praying, inhaling, exhaling. And just wait . . . by the second week, you'll have a very strong impulse to wave your hands in the air and shout with joy: "Look, Abba, no worries."

Wanting room to breathe is not only about actual breath, it is about a lack of space in the day, week, or phase of life to pause or to engage in activities that feed and fuel you. Expand your life to include your version of self-care and you'll create opportunities to expand your lungs with breaths of relief, joy, and satisfaction for a revived life. Stretch out on the couch for an afternoon of reading, prioritize workouts and exercise classes that reconnect you with your body and your breath, engage in fellowship, enjoy your yard or a nearby outdoor space, bake something that will delight the senses—the options are endless.

Ask for the peace
that surpasses
all understanding
to reunite your heart,
soul, and mind.

Care Package

Delivered to Your Heart

The package for you today includes a deflated balloon to remind you to breathe with intention. The next offering is the best sound machine imaginary money can buy. It will play whatever sound soothes you. (What sound would that be, by the way?) And I give to you a candle as a reminder of the light of God's love.

Explorations and Actions

What thought, person, or setting helps you breathe with ease?

_____

_____

Describe a time when you have felt God's peace.

_____

_____

_____

_____

_____

_____

_____

Go on a ten-minute prayer walk this week spending five minutes talking to God and five minutes listening. What is the first thing you will share with God?

_____

_____

_____

Revive the practices that nurture who you are at your core. List three activities and choose one to incorporate this week.

_____

_____

_____

God Sees Your Need

When peace is elusive, God is shaping you and giving you life.

> *The Spirit of God has made me, and the breath*
> *of the Almighty gives me life.*
>
> JOB 33:4 ESV

Self-Care Self Talk

Reconnecting with my breath and with the practices that soothe or energize me will reconnect me to God, the source of my breath, my life.

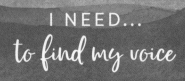

I NEED...
to find my voice

Did you try to speak up and nothing came out? Did thoughts storm and swirl in your mind for hours, practicing what you'd tell someone when the right moment came, and the right moment came and . . . nada. Zilch. You faked a cough.

I can relate. I have strong opinions and ideas that seem to fizzle when in a forum. And my mind and spirit are always collaborating on something creative. But when it's time to explain these imaginings, my mind decides that my verbal translation will never do justice to the ideation. I haven't faked a cough, but I'll use that trick.

Your voice is here. I promise you. It is merely muffled from residing beneath layers of memories, fears, limits set by others, stories you have rewritten over time, shyness, an inability to translate your boldness for the fainthearted, or wounds caused by past painful encounters.

What you have to share is important. You have a unique experience, mind, and history . . . and a one-of-a-kind take on life. You have something to say. Practice here today. I have prompts below for you to respond to out loud. This exercise might feel silly initially, but it will turn toward empowering when you realize your one-of-a-kind voice is ready to be heard. So ready.

Express yourself. State who you are and why your thoughts matter. What are ten words that describe you? Who is the you God made and deemed good and worthy?

Speak up for others. Lift your voice for those you want to defend and champion. What needs to be said? What truths need to be told? What did you not say on behalf of someone in the past that you want to declare now? Is there a bully in your midst? Say what too few are willing to say.

Rock the boat. I don't know what waters you are in or what kind of vessel you're paddling, but say what you really mean and what you believe. Do you feel judged by someone near or far (or even long gone) who squelches your opinions before they make it to the surface? You may have lost touch with what your opinion is because you surrendered it to keep the calm. Rock on.

Uncover what you have to say. What feelings or beliefs got drowned out by voices louder than yours and by voices magnified by hate or power? Were you ever so exhausted by the cacophony that you hit your own mute button? Flip the switch and let your voice ring out.

Share faith. Express wonder and awe. Take your spirit to open mic night and lift up praises. What is your testimony of being a beloved child of God? What do you wish others knew about grace and mercy? Close with "Can I get an amen?" The answer is yes, *amen*!

Sing, shout. Last round is all about declaring delight. You might have to holler the happy before you feel the happy. Do that right now. Bellow the bliss. Hooray! Cheers! Wahoo with wonder. Howl the gratitude.

Go through the list again to see what new words pour forth. Try it with a voice that is bolder and then discover the resonance true to your inner strength. Give life to the words in the depths of your stomach so they rise on your diaphragm and leap from your throat to your tongue and through your lips into the world. Phew. The physical journey of expression can override timidity and give force and weight to your words. Those precious, powerful, personal words.

You have a unique
experience, mind,
and history . . .
and a one-of-a-kind
take on life.
You have something
special to say.

Care Package

Delivered to Your Heart

I chose a comfy, fabulous T-shirt featuring an original quote from you (what might that be?). Next—surprise!—a microphone decorated with lots of bling. I hope you'll practice using your unique voice. Finally, I've included personalized cue cards for those moments of uncertainty when you need words and phrases that make sense. And cough drops—just in case.

Explorations and Actions

What do you want to say or need to say? What would motivate you to get it off your chest?

Everyone needs a mission statement. Write one or two paragraphs to help you own who you are and bring definition to your beliefs and purpose. Don't overthink it. You can refine it later.

_____

_____

Do you value your voice? How can you use it to make a difference, to encourage another, or to speak up in the presence of injustice?

_____

_____

Think of a time when you spoke up. How did it feel? What was the outcome?

_____

_____

God Sees Your Need

Be empowered by this truth: God listens to all you say and all your spirit longs to share. He will provide the opportunities and strength for you to speak with authenticity and power.

> *In the morning, LORD, you hear my voice; in the morning*
> *I lay my requests before you and wait expectantly.*
>
> PSALM 5:3

Self-Care Self Talk

When I speak up, I am accepting my value and adding an important voice to the world's song.

I NEED...
people

Finding our people is one of life's best discoveries. But when we are distanced from others emotionally or physically, we can feel untethered. If a good friend has moved recently or you've experienced the disconnection that occurs with busyness, you might feel restless. Are you grieving the loss of a loved one? Is a relationship strained and you're not sure where you stand?

I know the weight of loneliness when spending time alone is not by choice. Or when feelings of discouragement create a veil between me and others. Not being seen or understood is the most painful isolation.

I've invited you over for lemonade. We're sitting beneath my pergola and the breeze is warm and the sky is hazy. It feels good to be together talking about the importance of noticing the community that encircles and includes us in different ways. God gives us people. Our lives are enriched when we see them, receive them, and hold them as dear.

Camaraderie. Friends! Ah, so thankful for them. Tell me about some of your earliest friendships. What is the longest friendship you've maintained? Is there someone from days of old you might reach out to now? Those who have gone through circumstances and seasons with us become a part of our routine. Early schoolmates, college friends, coworkers, military comrades, fellow parents.

Church. Those who physically attend your church and those who are part of the larger body of Christ are all connected. Think of those you've had Bible studies with or prayed for. Consider the millions who face hardship and must persevere for their faith. Pray for those who feel outside of the church. May we embrace them and show God's love.

Community. Everyone you walk by and interact with at the grocery store, home store, theater, or the park is a person in your circle. It's just a bigger circle than you typically think of. Beyond your neighbors is a whole world of community folks you can include in your prayers: clerks, teachers, business owners and employees, baristas, civic leaders, service workers, students, kids, our society members who live on the streets.

Connection. People you meet through similar interests

can become kindred spirits. You might not have anything else in common, but no matter! You bond with one another through passions such as fitness training, reading, writing, food, humanitarian efforts, pets, music, movies, sports, and more.

Compassion. God trusts us and compels us to notice and care about others. Through this, we adopt a tenderness for those who are sick, looking for work, struggling with life, brokenhearted, kept on the sidelines, and anyone in need. Our capacity for compassion is inspired by advocates and individuals who are being a light in the world in their own special way. Those people are also a part of our circles because they beckon us to be our best.

Communion. These are individuals with whom we have deep, personal relationships. They know us the best and are intertwined with our histories in layered, complex ways. These are our family members, our spouse, and our children. They are the most familiar with our moods, flaws, strengths, and quirks, which makes their love all the more valued.

Every person can become one of our people when we hold them as a gift and are present to them when we see them, greet them, interact with them, or pray for them. This is how God will weave together your life with theirs. This is how God cares for the world.

God gives us people.
Our lives are enriched
when we see them,
receive them, and
hold them as dear.

Care Package

Delivered to Your Heart

Your gift is an appointment book to schedule get-togethers. A prayer journal to record the needs of others. And a beautiful wooden table that seats 12 so you can break bread with community.

Explorations and Actions

Praying for people draws us closer to them. Here is a brief prayer for each kind of relationship.

Camaraderie—God, give me a heart of gratitude for those who do life beside me.

Church—Lord, help me encourage my spiritual brothers and sisters.

Community—Jesus, may I see the specialness in each person I encounter and learn more about your character through them.

Connection—God, thank you for the fellowship of kindred spirits.

Communion—Please strengthen my union with those who are dearest to me. May I create conversations safe for vulnerability and authenticity.

Compassion—Creator, show me the brokenhearted. Reveal to me your love for those near and far so I am guided to pray, care, and act in your will.

God Sees Your Need

You are made to express love and your spirit is prepared for this.

> *A new commandment I give to you,*
> *that you love one another: just as I have loved you,*
> *you also are to love one another.*
>
> JOHN 13:34 ESV

Self-Care Self Talk

My need for people is an expression of God's hope. I will see and greet each person as a child of God.

I NEED...
a perspective shift

Remember when attitude adjustments were trendy? Maybe you had one or two. I know I did. And I nearly always ended up back where I started. Changing our response to what we see is an attitude adjustment and can be helpful. Changing how we see is a perspective shift—and can be life changing.

Your current perspective may have served you well through a recent season. Now you're bumping into its limitations and confronting its self-protective edges. You are stuck, frustrated, maybe even missing God's potential for you.

Here are three perspectives and possible shifts. See if one speaks to the change of perspective you are ready for.

Worn-Out Perspective

I have to earn peace and rest . . . maybe even goodness.

You strive to do all the right things. You probably tell yourself every other Tuesday that you can't earn grace. Still, you carry on at an unhealthy pace to gain fleeting moments of peace, when all along, beside you, is a pool of grace. It's time to shed confinements of self-criticism and fear and dive in.

New Perspective

God's grace covers me. It isn't for me to earn—
but to fall into with surrender and trust.

Worn-Out Perspective

I'm alone in this. Each time I give up control,
it feels like I am let down by everyone.

With the strength of self-sufficiency, you accept the challenge to go it alone—even though this has become a lonely practice. Explaining what needs to be done takes time and requires transparency, so you don't delegate the burden. When you have asked for help, you felt misunderstood or were disappointed with the result. God is bringing help to you. It is there now, in his power and through the hands and hearts of others. He is leading you to let go of outcomes and let in the blessings of asking, receiving, falling, and getting back up together.

New Perspective

I receive God's help coming from many places.
Connection is formed through vulnerability.

Worn-Out Perspective

I am faking my way through life.

You question whether you deserve what you have or the hope
you're holding onto. When you enter a conversation or a room,
your first impulse is to prove yourself rather than connect with
others. You don't believe it yet, but you are a noble treasure. As
is. If you're trying to earn a friendship or job you already have,
you're not trusting your instincts or gifting. Ask God to reveal his
unconditional view of you and your worth. Every flaw too. And
still, your authenticity as a loved child of God does not diminish.

New Perspective

I am made whole and holy by God. I am worthy of
this moment and my hope in the future.

Let in the blessings
of asking, receiving,
falling, and getting
back up together.

Care Package

Delivered to Your Heart

My gift to you includes rose-colored glasses, not so you can ignore reality but as a reminder that a new lens changes your outlook. Next . . . a piggy bank. Add money every time you default to the old perspective. Spend the money on something new, of course!

Explorations and Actions

Which of the worn-out perspectives most resonates with you?

_____

_____

Describe the last time you had this perspective.

_____

_____

Which of the new perspectives gives you a sigh of relief when you read it? Why?

_____

_____

Spend time thinking about why you might believe you need to earn peace, grace, or respect.

All three perspective scenarios shift from self-dependent to surrender. Which areas of your life are you resistant to surrender to God's care? Money, relationships, provision, career, future, children, spouse, joy, purpose, time, service . . . ?

_____

_____

_____

God Sees Your Need

Clinging to the security blanket of familiar ways is comfortable, but God nudges you toward transformation beyond the familiar.

> *Forget the former things; do not dwell on the past.*
> *See, I am doing a new thing! Now it springs up;*
> *do you not perceive it? I am making a way in*
> *the wilderness and streams in the wasteland.*
>
> ISAIAH 43:18-19

Self-Care Self Talk

Surrender is my RSVP to accept God's invitation to receive grace and help.

I NEED...
a motto

Did you select a word for the year during a New Year's Eve moment of anticipatory glee and an inner call to action? Keep that word written on your office whiteboard or painted on a stone that rests in the ceramic bowl that corrals your car keys. That word is and will continue to be encouraging. You just happen to be ready for more.

You, my friend, are ready for a motto. You don't have to have it printed on T-shirts or coffee cup sleeves for it to lift you up. When thoughts start to spiral or you are moving along with unsteady footing in unknown territory, a motto etched on the mind can eliminate distractions, calm the storm, and guide your focus back to your path.

I am pulling up a chair and I have my favorite notebook with me, the one with foldout pockets and zipper pouches in case we round up evidence of your life motivation. What truth compels you? What belief sustains you? What phrase serves as a laser beam cutting through the haze of vague platitudes, opinions, and judgments that fill social media outlets? What do you know to be true of God and his character? Did you tell yourself something over and over to endure a life trial in recent years?

A motto directs your heart's compass toward the same hope no matter the circumstance. You can use a Bible verse as your motto or as inspiration. Here are a few:

- "They who wait for the LORD shall renew their strength; they shall mount up with wings like eagles; they shall run and not be weary; they shall walk and not faint" (Isaiah 40:31 ESV).
- "He gives power to the weak and strength to the powerless" (Isaiah 40:29 NLT).
- "Rejoice always, pray without ceasing, in everything give thanks" (1 Thessalonians 5:16-18 NKJV).
- "When I am afraid, I put my trust in you" (Psalm 56:3 ESV).

Your motto might come to you through a thread of history. Is there a serious or silly family saying that has grown on you? A grandfather who survived his childhood dinner table with four hungry brothers may pass along a motto to his family: Savor your food as though there are never second helpings. That once-specific advice serves as a bigger-themed motto about enjoying the present moment and not counting on what comes next to satisfy.

Writer Anne Lamott explains that her book title *Bird by Bird* and its writing wisdom exist because she heard her dad offer this sage advice when her younger brother got overwhelmed doing a report on birds. The whole of the task was daunting. But when their father said to move forward "bird by bird," it was permission to invest in one small step. While the finished report was the goal, the most important task was to craft the foundational blocks of information. This wisdom would be a helpful motto (a Lamotto, actually!) for times when we're at a stress-induced standstill.[2]

Do you have your motto? I'll have my pen ready to write down your response. Imagine this scene. Someone comes to you and asks to chat. They say they've noticed how you do life and love with an impressionable peace and strength. Now they want to know, for their own journey, if you could give them words to live by. You take a deep breath and you say . . . ?

2 Anne Lamott, *Bird by Bird*, (New York: Anchor Books, 2019), 18.

A motto etched
on the mind can

eliminate distractions,

calm the storm,

and guide your focus

back to your path.

Care Package

Delivered to Your Heart

I want you to have my favorite thesaurus so you can find the perfect words. I've included a bracelet with your motto engraved on it. And I hired a biographer to follow you around and film how you live your motto.

Explorations and Actions

What is a motto you want to claim for your life journey?

_____

_____

How have words shaped your confidence, faith, or identity?

_____

_____

Which words hold a lot of power for you?

_____

Who in your life frequently gives you words of encouragement?

_____

_____

Consider sending them a handwritten letter or offering to them a motto written on a pretty notecard.

Create a prayer to say upon waking each day so your first words are offerings to God. What might that prayer be?

God Sees Your Need

When our desire is to illuminate what is good and holy, God will give us the words and the foundation to stand upon so we can speak with conviction and hope.

> *Let the words of my mouth and the meditation of*
> *my heart be acceptable in your sight, O LORD,*
> *my rock and my redeemer.*
>
> PSALM 19:14 ESV

Self-Care Self Talk

I am seen and heard. What I say and the words I live out each day matter.

I NEED...
a day off

've cleared your schedule. I had to make some calls and do some rearranging. I may have told someone that you moved to a foreign land. I hope that is okay. I am determined for you to have a day off. I have the impression that if you stumbled upon a genie in a bottle and were granted three wishes, you would have used one for this simple and not-so-simple request. That is how precious a free day can be.

You smile in anticipation of what you might do with this day. Nobody will be judging you if you sleep in, get up, and go back to bed with a good book and a stack of Oreos.

We rarely give ourselves the expanse of a day lived our way. If we have a morning to ourselves that isn't consumed with work or previous obligations, we're apologetic if that time isn't devoted to productivity in some form. This day off is an experiment. A practice run (or stay, as the case may be). Maybe you lost the self-care skill in the process of acquiring the skills the world deems necessary: setting notifications for appointments, checking on others via social media when you wish someone would check in with you in real time, mapping your days down to the minute, saying yes to something that will drain your energy . . .

What will your day look like, feel like? Consider this:

Do you want the day planned or to flow with in-the-moment wants and whims?

Do you want time with others or time solo?

Entertainment? Settle into a movie theater with a sigh as the lights dim and a story unfolds. Or attend a play, concert, festival, community event.

Allow your body to move and stretch. Tell it you love it and are grateful for how it serves you.

Do you want stillness to pray, meditate, journal, or to listen to God's sweet somethings?

Music . . . oh, yes. Build a playlist that lifts your mood, inspires creativity, or soothes your soul.

Do you want deep conversations right now or silly ones with healing laughter?

You might crave an afternoon of play, telling jokes, and building forts with your child.

Shop downtown with friends or shop online while you eat mac and cheese.

Sit on the porch swing with your spouse and sip lemonade.

Maybe you'll create something you saw on a cooking show. (In this scenario, someone else will clean the kitchen, I'm sure of it.)

If you do sit in bed and read, what would you read? You can send me out to buy a stack of magazines with topics to suit your mood. What will it be? Spiritual health, home design, arts and crafts, nature?

Free yourself from setting goals. May these ideas serve to remind you that a day can be anything you want. Give yourself the time to rediscover who you are and nurture the ideas, loves, and longings that make you, you. Open your arms and life to receive gifts that will serve you well beyond 24 hours: refreshment, grace, movement, clarity, peace.

Give yourself the
time to rediscover who
you are and nurture
the ideas, loves,
and longings that
make you, you.

Care Package

Delivered to Your Heart

You are ready for a free day. This special delivery has a small pewter bell you can ring for service. (I can't guarantee anyone will come, but it's nice to pretend!) Next, you'll find slippers for your overworked feet and a cozy robe that has a pocket with the word "worthy" embroidered on it.

Explorations and Actions

Describe your ideal free day.

_____

_____

_____

_____

_____

How did you experience joy and renewal as a kid?

_____

_____

_____

_____

What one activity or inactivity could you incorporate, in some version, into daily life to experience regular refreshment?

_____

_____

_____

What are you giving great importance that may be causing your life to skew toward unhealthy?

_____

_____

_____

_____

God Sees Your Need

Allowing for healthy rest and margins of unplanned time is how you make time to receive God's refreshment.

> *I will refresh the weary and satisfy the faint.*
>
> JEREMIAH 31:25

Self-Care Self Talk

This rest is not selfish, it is soulful. It draws me to the well of well-being—God's love and care.

I NEED...
a pep talk

t's been one of those down days. You're forgetting who you are and what you are capable of. You want to pull the covers up over your head for a nap that carries you through to tomorrow or scroll online until you find a dramedy series you can watch numbly. Maybe you are tempted to quit a project that you started with such gusto it physically pains you to imagine putting it on hold and equally pains you to keep going. You've been doing so much it is no wonder you are ready for a pep talk.

Cheer is here.

I want to remind you who you are and how there is provision in the works and a path unfolding even when you cannot see it. Settle in for story time, because I am going to tell you a bit about yourself.

You are kind. Your ability to discern when a friend needs a good word or a simple gift is uncanny. Even when you are running at a pace that is beyond your reserves, you notice the needs around you and stop to help when you stop for very little else.

You are a shining star. Others are inspired when they witness you and your faith. Your times of weariness only make you more endearing to those friends and family, because they realize you are fueled by hope in the Lord instead of superhuman genes.

You are true. When others are tempted to fake it until they make it, you move in the world from a place of truth. What you don't know, you will learn or trust in the strength of others. What you don't see, you place in God's hands for care and once there, they are no longer magnified uncertainties, they are manageable factors known and tended to by him.

You are brave. Those bold leaps you make start with a sprig of green hope budding inside you. The light in your eyes comes on the moment it is time to reap the joy of faithful forward motion. You aren't reckless with important next steps. You gather strength and seek wisdom from God.

You are human. Maybe you did forget this during the planning, juggling, serving, and even the praying. The divine hand of God is not moving across the page of a ledger that tracks productivity or popularity. There is not a minus sign made in red ink because you needed a day or a stretch of those days to express your doubts.

You are loved. Unconditionally loved, my friend. Breathe into that eternal truth with soul-deep relief and belief. Greeting cards express a love that stretches to the moon and back. That's not the half of it. You are loved to the heart of God and back. You are wrapped in eternal grace. There is not a contract with teeny tiny print listing reasons that love could be revoked. Uh-uh. The unbreakable covenant with Jesus covers and carries you.

Did you see yourself in these words? Was your spirit restored and your hope refreshed? Whether you needed a pep talk today to get through an immediate endeavor or to face a year of change, I pray you have received the gift of assurance. If you still want to watch those shows or take a nap, do that. I hope you have a cozy blanket nearby too. God will oversee your circumstances and bring cheer to your spirit.

There is provision
in the works and a
path unfolding
even when you
cannot see it.

Care Package

Delivered to Your Heart

I want you to feel the love. This care package includes a comforting blanket to draw around your shoulders as you take in encouraging words. I give you a scroll that lists all the ways you have been and are amazing. Lastly, here are a pair of ruby slippers to serve as a reminder that you shine when you stand in your authenticity.

Explorations and Actions

Which of the six statements about you resonates the most with you today and why?

_____

_____

_____

What brings you cheer? What discourages you?

_____

_____

_____

Choose to reach out to someone this week for cheerful connection or to serve another and shift your focus toward the joy of giving.

Return to a sense of yourself. Finish the phrase "I am . . ." ten times.

_____

_____

_____

_____

_____

_____

_____

_____

God Sees Your Need

Don't default to rote thoughts that discourage. Listen closely for what God is wanting to share.

> *Call to me and I will answer you, and will tell you great and hidden things that you have not known.*
>
> JEREMIAH 33:3 ESV

Self-Care Self Talk

When I need encouragement or rest, it isn't a sign of defeat; it means I am carefully listening to my life and responding with wisdom.

I NEED...
a stunt double

You've faced some tricky situations, moments of daring living, and more than a few gravity-defying leaps of faith. It's no wonder you'd like a stand-in to go into the fray on your behalf. This real-life stuff can be quite dangerous for the fragile beings we are. I confess, it would be nice to make that call when risks of pain, exposure of my faults, or rejection loom.

Where would you send your stunt double while you rearrange closets, watch movies, or attend a concert? They could go to a family gathering and save you from the landmines of rehashed arguments or strained relationships. They could take a call for you and endure the crushing weight of bad news. Let them dangle midair when you are overwhelmed and hanging on by a thread. Give this daredevil understudy their big moment to play you through the mildly bumpy knowns, the scary knowns, and those wildly terrifying, fully imagined unknowns.

You and I want to map out what might happen to antici-pate the twists and turns that could send us skidding round tight corners of harm and along edges of humility. This seems so smart at the time. Who doesn't want protection from anything that hurts? Yet, if our true selves only made appearances for photo op moments when we receive accolades, cross finish lines, hold the newborn, ride the adrenaline of a new love, and share dramatic embraces of hello, we wouldn't have the wisdom, compassion, or perseverance of faith we gather through false starts, grief, heartbreak, injustice, and goodbyes.

Turns out, vulnerability is how we grow and become the child of God we're meant to be. It is better to become refined through the pressure of integrity than it is to be formed by the pressure to be perfect. Knowing this doesn't make life easier, but it does free you to live your extraordinary, one-of-a-kind adven-ture as *you*. Facing the fires without a lookalike backup invites you to trust God completely and to trust those around you to ex-tend grace and a helping hand when you are headed for a crash.

I'm not officially trained as a stunt double; however, here are a few things I can do:

- cheer you on while you train for something like an upcoming speaking engagement or a race

- role play as your boss as you practice asking for a promotion or sharing your big idea
- tell you the truth about how great you are and when you have kale in your teeth
- be your warm-up act if you share your life through self-deprecating one-liners as a comedian
- listen to you when you share about your fear of being vulnerable
- laugh with you when you share about that time you felt foolish but got a glimpse of how freeing it is to not care what others think
- celebrate with you approaching the next unknown with vulnerability and openness
- remind you and myself that God is going before us and covering us in his peace

God has already mapped and taken notes for what lies ahead and what you need. The challenges will still befall you, but your vulnerability of spirit will allow you to discern the spiritual guidance, comfort, and encouragement. No safety nets. No stand-ins. Because where God is leading you, my friend, is better than a Hollywood ending; it's a holy eternity.

It is better to become refined through the pressure of integrity than it is to be formed by the pressure to be perfect.

Care Package

Delivered to Your Heart

My gifts today include a helmet to protect your thoughts from fear. Next is a heart-shaped piece of jade—a durable stone to remind you of your strength when feeling fragile. Last gift . . . a mirror so you can look at the face of one who has overcome the challenges of being human and expressing who they are—the ultimate act of bravery.

Explorations and Actions

What challenge, discomfort, or sorrow do you wish you could avoid right now? What is giving you strength to continue?

_____

_____

_____

Have you had to be strong for another person? If so, your impulse to be in control might be heightened. To release that, write your need for help as a prayer.

_____

_____

_____

What remarkable stunt have you pulled off? Describe an example of your perseverance, cleverness, fortitude, faithfulness, or vulnerability.

_____

_____

_____

_____

_____

_____

_____

God Sees Your Need

What's better than a stunt double? A loving God who goes before you in all situations and speaks assurances over you.

It is the LORD who goes before you. He will be with you; he will not leave you or forsake you. Do not fear or be dismayed.

DEUTERONOMY 31:8 ESV

Self-Care Self Talk

I will stand up to my fear with the assurance of faith, the comfort of hope, and the strength of surrender.

I NEED...
a day at the beach

This is for all those times you've said under your breath, "This is no day at the beach." Today, you get to change that. I've made all the arrangements. Hop into the Jeep. Your driver is taking you to a stretch of coastline where you can just be and breathe.

After an exhilarating ride with the windows down, the driver parks along a narrow country road. You get out of the car and finger-comb your windswept hair. Steps away is a beach trail sign by a small grove of trees. The driver motions for you to keep going and says he'll bring whatever is in the car.

You whisper a quick prayer for soul refreshment and walk beneath the arch of tree branches and journey along the sandy path. There's a craggy piece of driftwood—the perfect bench to sit and kick off your shoes and roll up your T-shirt sleeves. Then you rise and continue around the curve and into a scene from a postcard. With arms stretched wide, you take in a deep breath of nature's sea-spray infuser. Splashing along the water's edge is a must. You rush to greet the surf. Your toes are ready to feel the sting of cold water; your feet ready for the challenge to keep you upright when the wave recedes with force.

A shell catches your attention and you scoop it out of the water. It's the kind scattered all over the beach, but the abundance makes it no less exquisite. The pearly interior with a translucent hint of rainbow colors. The deep blue-black exterior with spirals drawn by nature. You cup this prize with both hands and gaze at it while you walk, mesmerized by the blessing of intimately holding beauty while also surrounded by it.

A rushing inlet is your boundary. You turn to wander back alongside the quickly disappearing impressions your feet made on the way to the inlet. They look like quotation marks just waiting for a proclamation to embrace. "Make a note: I was here!" you say aloud.

Your timing is perfect. Goodies have been set up for you: a large striped blanket and pillow and a picnic lunch of juicy red grapes, artisan bread, local cheeses, sparkling water, and your favorite dessert. There's a quilted beach bag with a note from me that reads: "Breathe in the refreshment and bring it back with you." Inside, I placed a saltwater-taffy-colored journal and pen and a slim volume of poetry inspired by the ocean. You hug the gifts to your chest. Your afternoon is lazy and lush. You dine on tangy words and sweet fruit, both sating your once weary soul.

Your delight invites thoughts of friends who would love this beach. *This should have been a family trip or friends' getaway!* That desire to share is so you, but right now it's important to be you with you. To be you with the gulls and the tumbling sea foam. To be you dozing in the sun. To be you with God and his intricately designed and beloved creation (of which you are a part). To be you on a quiet beach guarded by mounds of sea grass waving in the breeze.

You wave back.

The driver thinks you're beckoning him. He hurries over and asks, "Are you ready to head home?"

"No. Not yet. I need to be here a bit longer. There's more for me to gather before I go."

Your afternoon is
lazy and lush.
You dine on tangy
words and sweet fruit,
both sating your
once weary soul.

Care Package

Delivered to Your Heart

My presents for you today are in a white tote bag with wavy blue stripes. There is a sea-blue Mason jar filled with shells and stones. And a copy of *Gift from the Sea* by Anne Morrow Lindbergh is tucked in a white cotton sun hat.

Explorations and Actions

The ocean is mesmerizing and mysterious. Recall a time when you experienced the untamed mystery of faith. Did you feel exhilarated, scared, free, small, powerful . . . ?

_____

_____

_____

What feelings arose during today's offering? What part of the beach day experience did your spirit need?

_____

_____

_____

_____

Even without a beach, what might you do today to have communion with God?

_____

_____

Hold and stare at one item of beauty today. How might its beauty represent your beauty within?

_____

_____

God Sees Your Need

God's vast love and wisdom rush onto the shore of your soul. And when you awaken from a time of emotional distance or spiritual slumber, you are still in God's endless presence.

> _How precious also are Your thoughts to me, O God!_
> _How great is the sum of them! If I should count them,_
> _they would be more in number than the sand;_
> _when I awake, I am still with You._
>
> PSALM 139:17-18 NKJV

Self-Care Self Talk

I am held by God as a beautiful treasure. God's wild creation invites me to dive into the mystery of faith.

I NEED...
a thing, my thing

I envision us at a dinner party. We're seated around an elegant table with elegant people, and being served decadent appetizers on tiny plates. It is all lovely. Until the guest seated next to you turns to you and says, "So what is your passion? Your purpose? Your thing?" I'm mid-chew, or I would respond, "Shouldn't you wait until the entrée to pose such a meaty question to my friend?"

You ask if the chatty guest will excuse us and you motion for me to join you in the hallway. Why does this question set off the flashing panic lights? Because it matters. I have some smaller questions that might help you come up with your response:

What activities and ideas occupied your time and energy in childhood and young adulthood? By looking at your earliest interests, you can see what fascinated you naturally. Was there anything you did that would cause you to lose track of time because you were so focused on it?

Is one of those a part of your life now? If yes, in what form is that interest still active? Is this something you might want to invest more effort into? If no, what has taken the place of those early interests?

What do others say you're good at? This can be a strong indicator of your strengths and purpose. Maybe you are a great planner, a great organizer, a creative thinker, a problem solver, an advocate, a listener. Pay attention to what people are telling you about you.

What is the thing about which you say "Some year I will do_____," but you don't follow through? Even though you aren't doing this thing, it still could indicate your *thing*. How does it make you feel when you consider fulfilling this rather than delaying it? Would you describe it as a goal, a dream, a fantasy, a longing, a bucket-list priority?

Now come up with a way to move toward this thing gently or boldly.

Take a proactive step toward it.

What is one small step of commitment you can take toward that thing? Maybe you will stop looking at online course catalogs and fill out a college application instead.

Pursue a modified version of it.

If you view your interest as an all-or-nothing pursuit, you might be keeping it at a distance so you don't have to commit to it or fail trying. Shake up your comfort zone by doing a version of what scares you. For example, if you've daydreamed about creating gardens for a living, what modified version can honor your desire and ability? You could sign up to oversee a local community garden. You could tell neighbors you're available for hire to help plan and plant their gardens next season.

Do the thing.

No cushions or comfort-zone buffers here. Take the leap. How does it make you feel to consider finally pursuing your heart thing? No, wait . . . "consider" is language of delay. You are doing this thing. It is in you and a part of you. God has placed this on your spiritual radar for a long time. No time like the present to state this publicly.

I bow in admiration as you walk past me and back to your seat. I sit down and lean in to hear what you have to say. You turn to the curious guest and say:

My heart passion is _____.

I express it to the world by _____.

Take the leap.
How does it make
you feel to consider
finally pursuing your
heart thing?

Care Package

Delivered to Your Heart

The first gift is a portable watercolor paint set so you can be ready for creative expression. And I've included a kit to grow an herb garden. As you nurture plants, they will sprout and produce. The same is true when you nurture your purpose.

Explorations and Actions

List your gifts and strengths. Which one brings great joy and satisfaction? How can you grow it, use it, and make it a part of your daily life?

_____

_____

_____

_____

Describe when you felt compelled from within toward an activity, purpose, mission, or cause. What might this reveal about your purpose?

_____

_____

_____

_____

Try something new each month. Learn to dance, paint, knit, golf, speak a new language, play an instrument—anything you're curious about. A passion might be revealed.

What have you delayed doing that might be related to your purpose? Write a vow to look past fear or excuses to the possibility.

_____

_____

_____

God Sees Your Need

God knows you are searching and wants you to trust that he's working through you always.

> *It is God who works in you to will and to act in order to fulfill his good purpose.*
>
> PHILIPPIANS 2:13

Self-Care Self Talk

God has given me every good and perfect gift. It is up to me how I use these gifts to find fulfillment and bless others.

I NEED...
a spiritual retreat

Y ou don't have to get away to have a spiritual retreat. We'll hang out at your house. Later, you can do this on your own in some cabin with a fireplace, porch, soft down quilts, and a rocking chair facing the mountains. (That sounds nice. Maybe I'll be two cabins over.)

Stand with me. Let's shrug and then relax our shoulders a few times, close our eyes, and tilt our heads gently side to side. Now let's shake our limbs and shake off our stress, daily routines, and anything that distracts. (You can confirm your dentist appointment tomorrow.)

Before we pray, let's draw in and release our breath and mentally repeat these phrases for several rounds: *I breathe in God's peace, I breathe out love. I breathe in God's hope, I breathe out compassion.*

Pray with me: *Lord, we're thankful for this time dedicated* to seeking you and knowing you better. May we offer ourselves fully and listen deeply to all you speak to our spirits and show our minds. Amen.

God Is . . .

Let's share what we know of God. For the next several minutes, we'll say "God is . . ." followed by whatever comes to mind. Here are some of mine: God is with me. God is generous. God is surprising. God is compassionate. God is creative. God is with us.

Walking with God

Walk with slow half-steps in a circle or up and down the hallway or yard for 15 minutes. This is an enriching practice. While walking, choose a phrase from this verse or a phrase of your own to meditate on.

"Trust in the LORD with all your heart, and do not lean on your own understanding. In all your ways acknowledge him, and he will make straight your paths" (Proverbs 3:5-6 ESV).

Meeting God

Journal for 20 to 30 minutes about these: Describe your first impression of God. How do you sense God's presence in your life now? How has your relationship changed over time? What do you know about God now that you did not understand before?

Trusting God

Do not fear, for I have redeemed you; I have summoned you by name; you are mine. When you pass through the waters, I will be with you; and when you pass through the rivers, they will not sweep over you. When you walk through the fire, you will not be burned; the flames will not set you ablaze . . . Since you are precious and honored in my sight, and because I love you (Isaiah 43:1-2,4).

Let's journey through this passage mindfully. What feeling emerges when you think of God calling you by name? What life "river" have you passed through? What "fire" has threatened but not burned you? In what ways do you experience God's love?

Offering

I place a cobalt blue ceramic bowl in the center of the table. On pieces of paper, we'll draw symbols to represent our personal offerings, and we'll place them in the bowl. Here are mine: open hands (service), an ear (listening), feet (following daily), a broken heart (surrendering losses). Then we'll draw a symbol of what we sense God is giving us. I draw a full cup of water to represent endless refreshment. What is God giving to you for spiritual nourishment?

I breathe in God's peace,

I breathe out love.

I breathe in God's hope,

I breathe out compassion.

Care Package

Delivered to Your Heart

I want you to have a retreat any time you desire. Here is some fabric to drape over a table and colored glass stones to scatter for light and beauty. Verses written on individual cards are provided to help you choose a theme or to use for your walking meditation times.

Explorations and Actions

What do you know about God from your own journey and relationship with him?

_____

_____

_____

_____

Do a walking meditation and then record the thoughts and feelings that came up. Was there a point when you shifted from being self-conscious to being at ease and contemplative?

_____

_____

What offering do you make today to God and what do you sense you are receiving from God?

_____

_____

_____

_____

Set a date for a personal spiritual retreat in the next few weeks. Enjoy the process of planning which elements you will include from this example or what you will create for your version.

God Sees Your Need

God will be present in the intentional spaces you create for communion and intimacy.

> *Draw near to God, and he will draw near to you.*
>
> JAMES 4:8 ESV

Self-Care Self Talk

When I devote time to be with God, my priorities are rearranged for the better.

I NEED...
straight talk

I t is scary to ask someone to shed light on who we are. Even when we aren't asking for personal revelation, we encounter self-awareness when we are in community and pay attention. Everyday moments chatting with and bumping into other personalities expose our areas of lack or resistance. Discomfort as well as zealous confidence can point to areas in which we need to grow, bend, soften, expand, reduce, step aside, push through, stand strong, or set boundaries.

You and I are on this brief journey that goes to the deep places quickly. While I can't be the one who can tell you about you, I can invite you to illuminate your life in this safe space.

I know what it is to have hang-ups, insecurities, doubts, and gifts so engrained that I cannot separate fact from fiction, helpful from the hurtful, or even the crushing-it moments from the cringeworthy ones. If you're ready for it, these straight-talk questions will help you see yourself with open eyes and notice what you may be overlooking that could become an open door to deeper authenticity and freedom.

- What are your two most restrictive insecurities?
- What is the root fear that, at times, holds you back from being authentic? You honor the God who made you by sharing who you truly are with more people.
- What are you good at? The bright green buds of our gifting can be hindered when someone around us didn't or doesn't honor it. Shine light on these abilities and foster their growth.
- What actions or circumstances trigger your anger? How has anger served you? Hurt you or others?
- Listen up. There's a story you tell about yourself that needs to be deconstructed. Whether this is a story of greatness or lameness, pare away the non-fruit-bearing tendrils and grow something true.
- You have a pet peeve. If you examine it closely, does it relate to something that bothers you about yourself or that someone used to judge about you?
- When you are lonely, are you missing a part of yourself?

A sense of God's presence? Or the companionship of a certain person? (There are no wrong answers.)

- You may have a bias that sways your choices, decisions, interactions, fears, responses, and faith. Notice which of your defaults is based on a bias toward people, places, or perspectives. When we rely on automatic responses, we risk living a limited and limiting life.

- There's an aspect of you that you protect and are defensive about when anyone steps too close to it. What is it and when did you start to build a wall around it?

- Which is a stronger motivation for you lately? Comparison or compassion? Empathy or envy?

- In what way do you limit God's healing and power to fuel your life?

We are complex beings. God didn't slap us together without intention. Even when it is uncomfortable, we become intimately twined with our Creator while exploring how we're personally crafted and how experiences have shaped us.

Honor it all—the mess, mystery, and mercy form the blessing God sends into the world through you. I'm just telling it to you straight.

We became intimately twined with our Creator while exploring how we're personally crafted.

Care Package

Delivered to Your Heart

I gift to you a lamp to illuminate those dark spaces that keep you from venturing into the unknown. A long lunch with a cherished friend who allows you to share openly and offers wise counsel. And a plaque that reads "Tell Yourself the Truth—You Are Worth It!" for moments when doubt invades your thoughts.

Explorations and Actions

What insecurity pulls you away from behaving or living authentically?

_____

_____

_____

When have you downplayed a strength? Why might you struggle to champion yourself?

_____

_____

_____

_____

What do you need to deal with before you can move forward? A past hurt, a failure, a relationship, the need for control? Ask God to help you see your way beyond this obstacle.

Which of the questions presented in the offering gave you the strongest insight today? Why?

God Sees Your Need

He is so much a part of us that it is truly astonishing. God's desire is that we rest in the transformation that happens to us the more we embrace his presence in our lives.

> *The human spirit is a lamp of the LORD that*
> *sheds light on one's inmost being.*
>
> PROVERBS 20:27

Self-Care Self Talk

Honesty with myself and others is a vital step toward becoming the person God created me to be.

I NEED...
a love letter

Dear One,

I am filled with joy each time I see you and your unique strength and wonder. When you think nobody is noticing how you make your way through the day, I witness your grace when you engage with someone in need. With pride, I have watched you step beyond intimidation to be strong for a person who was not and could not be strong in a difficult time.

There is so much to love about you.

I've heard you encourage a friend who was trying to make sense of the way life unfolded. You grabbed her hand and held it to express understanding. Never once did you force an explanation or give her meaningless words. You are too wise and too good to do that to someone. Your faith allowed you to be with her in the questions and uplift her with prayer and words of courage.

When you entered the world, it became a brighter place

of possibility. Strangers could see the light in your eyes as you became you. When discouragements got you down, the courage within your spirit did not cower. You rallied with faith and were emboldened by a bravery of the soul to show up.

You use your gifts with an ease that few have. I know you want a more solidified sense of calling. That will come in time. Be hopeful while waiting for a next step. You are getting to know the wonder of who you are and how God made you. All the pieces aren't yet fitting together in your mind. They are fitting together in God's hand and plan. Can you trust that?

A previous stumble is still causing you frustration. Maybe even embarrassment. You do know that you aren't perfect and never will be, right? Why are you shocked when this is proven by innocent mistakes as well as big blunders? You are too hard on yourself. You've been entering the chaos of the world with your chin up. Sometimes your guard is up too. You don't always have to be strong.

I'm grateful to come alongside you and place a protective arm around your shoulders when you feel vulnerable or burdened. I stand and watch you take steps forward even when you're scared. There are times you hold back because you are discerning and measured. Wisdom looks good on you. Stand tall with gratitude when you look back over your life and notice the ways you have grown. You are not a fading flower, my dear. You are a sequoia. Your top branches will reach beyond your own line of sight and you will provide shelter and wonder to others during your lifetime.

When the furrow in your brow is showing more often than your smile, that's about the time you encounter a challenge that makes you throw your arms in the air to surrender what you cannot do in your own power. And then it happens . . . that laugh. You laugh because this experience is more familiar than you want it to be. You've been here before and God provided for you, redirected or carried you, or caught you when you fell. Not many people see the joy in this, but you do. It makes me so happy that you do.

You are held dear as beloved. This isn't good-bye because my love letter to you goes on and on.

Forever,

Love

Be hopeful while waiting for a next step. You are getting to know the wonder of who you are and how God made you.

Care Package

Delivered to Your Heart

I've imagined a bundle to inspire letter writing. I want you to have an Italian glass fountain pen and a jar of indigo ink. Monogrammed stationery is a must. It will be delivered in a soft shade of your favorite color. I include red wax and a heart-shaped stamp to seal your next letter with love.

Explorations and Actions

Which part of the love letter spoke to you today and why?

_____

_____

_____

Describe an earlier time when you could've used a love letter. Write that letter now to yourself in the past. Offer healing words.

_____

_____

_____

_____

_____

Is loving others easier or harder for you than receiving love?

_____

Who in your life could use a love letter? Consider writing one a month to send to a friend, family member, or someone you admire.

_____

_____

_____

God Sees Your Need

Notice how you are cared for throughout the day. Receive the words and actions that fill you with a sense of being loved as a child of God.

> *See what great love the Father has lavished on us,*
> *that we should be called children of God!*
> *And that is what we are!*
>
> 1 John 3:1

Self-Care Self Talk

Each day is a new love letter from my Creator. How I live it is my love letter back to God.

I NEED...
time travel

Taking a trip down memory lane can shed light on who we are and who God is. This also helps us have empathy and appreciation for where we stand today. Envisioning the future is an exercise in hypotheticals, yet this too can tell us about our needs and longings and fears in the now.

A special time-travel transport device isn't necessary. Let's spend some time doing good ol' reminiscing and imagining.

To the Past

You have yearbooks spread out on the dining table. In a basket are ticket stubs, journals, notes from friends, drawings, seventh-grade homework, and trinkets. Some make you smile; others remind you of difficult times. Look at your journey with hindsight clarity.

- What is your first memory of feeling strong? Loved?
- Describe a difficult time during which you experienced

injustice. How is God's presence evident in hindsight?

- Imagine you get one do-over. What would it be?
- View the people who were part of your spiritual and personal journey. Who do you wish you had shown appreciation for at the time?
- Which friends made you feel seen and loved?
- At age six, what did you like best about yourself? Age fourteen? Age twenty-one?
- What four words describe younger you?

To the Future

Only God knows what the future landscape of our days will be. We're not here to cast predictions; instead, we'll look at what your hope is for the future.

- What have you finally allowed yourself to do or be?
- You figure out something important about who you are at your core: What might that be?
- What do you think your top three priorities are in the future?
- What adventure have you possibly pursued as a result of a greater trust in the Lord?
- You are free from:

- What four words describe future you?
- You are most grateful for:

Back to the Present

We stand at home base again. Now. It's the only moment that can be a living offering to God. It is refreshing to look back and ahead and to bring insights to the present day.

- What can you do today to honor your past self and your future self?
- How do you want to deepen your spiritual life now?
- What did you lose along the way and gain along the way?
- What new thing do you want to start doing today so it is a part of your future?
- When reviewing the past and imagining the future, did you have a sense of urgency about any part of your life?
- What about your past makes you tender toward yourself now?
- What about your possible future makes you most thankful for God's faithfulness?

Friend, I pray you can appreciate your unique pilgrimage. The only item on your travel itinerary today is to stand in your now with gratitude.

Now.
It's the only
moment that can
be a living
offering to God.

Care Package

Delivered to Your Heart

Here is your new gift. A shadow box for gathering special mementos from your past. Next year's calendar to plan the important things you want to accomplish and moments you don't want to miss. And a time capsule for you to fill now with notes, writings, and memorabilia. You don't have to bury this one. Just set it aside in a closet or on a shelf and pick a date to open it.

Explorations and Actions

What would you tell eighteen-year-old you? How would you share this insight or knowledge with a young family member or friend who's just starting into adulthood?

How has your past helped shape the person you are today?

_____

_____

What gives you the most confidence about the future?

_____

_____

What is one thing you discovered or recalled today that empowers you in the present?

_____

_____

God Sees Your Need

God is the author of your story and is eager to be a part of each day and decade. You can entrust your future to his love.

> *She is clothed with strength and dignity,*
> *and she laughs without fear of the future.*
>
> PROVERBS 31:25 NLT

Self-Care Self Talk

God was with me. I stand on that truth today to savor this moment, witness my growth, and embrace people and circumstances with faith.

I NEED...
a windfall

Wouldn't it be grand if you could expect to receive a treasure during your lifetime? Imagine getting a special delivery with a letter of inheritance from a generous neighbor you knew when you were five. Or you enter an international talent contest and take the cash prize with your rendition of *You Are My Sunshine* on the harmonica. I had no idea you played.

Reflecting on a fictional financial windfall might seem like an indulgent money trail of thought, but the flipside of that coin is that you can intentionally explore how a perspective of plenty changes your outlook. Respond to these questions about priorities, joy, needs, and wants and you will discover what you hold dear in want or plenty.

What is the very first thing you would do?

Who would you call right away for advice?

What debt would you settle immediately?

How and what would you give to God?

What family needs would you be thrilled to take care of?

How would you invest in your health and wellness?

Who would you first give money to?

What object would you buy first?

What would you get rid of?

Would you keep your current job?

What fears might this windfall alleviate?

Does this change your sense of God's provision?

Is there something seemingly small but meaningful you would get for you or a loved one?

Which nonprofits would you donate to and why?

Who would you splurge on first . . . and what would you buy them?

What destination trip would be at the top of your list?

How would you set aside funds for the future?

What fear might be sparked by having wealth?

What way of spending or using the money would be the most joyful?

Who would you surprise with a special delivery of a big check and why?

What would you do as a vocation if pay was no longer a factor?

What would be a cherished gift to receive if you had enough money to buy anything?

Did any of your answers surprise you?

That's a lot of questions. I'll ask just one more: What keeps you from living with this sense of abundance today? Because that part is real.

You have the abundance of God's provision, which reaches far beyond savings accounts and dream trips. "Whoever can be trusted with very little can also be trusted with much, and whoever is dishonest with very little will also be dishonest with much" (Luke 16:10). God has entrusted you with a little in some ways and a lot in others. How you live honestly and authentically with those blessings, talents, resources, friendships, opportunities, and dreams is what creates true abundance. Let's not allow a spirit of frugality stop us from giving when we feel led or walking with faith in the direction of dreams planted in our very souls.

You have the
abundance of
God's provision,
which reaches far
beyond savings accounts
and dream trips.

Care Package

Delivered to Your Heart

This gift would not be complete without at least $100,000 (Monopoly money, but it's the thought that counts). I'm giving you a money bag to fill with notes of gratitude. A small fountain that flows at all hours is given as a reminder of God's endless provision.

Explorations and Actions

Describe a time you have experienced a sense of abundance.

In what ways do you respond to life with a spirit of frugality? How might a shift in perspective result in a shift in circumstances?

What area of lack or loss do you bring to God today?

_____

_____

_____

_____

Go about your entire week as though you have received a huge windfall. See how it changes your attitude and your ability to give, serve, and stop keeping a ledger sheet of what others have.

God Sees Your Need

When God calls us to give, it isn't because he doesn't see our need, it is because he wants our needs filled with spiritual abundance. We experience plenty when faithfulness is a priority.

Honor the LORD with your wealth, with the firstfruits of all your crops; then your barns will be filled to overflowing, and your vats will brim over with new wine.

PROVERBS 3:9-10

Self-Care Self Talk

Hope and compassion prepare me to be a vessel that receives and gives with a sense of plenty.

I NEED...
a happy place

Where is your happy place? Have you always wanted one, or did a wise friend notice your stress level was rising and ever so casually suggest that you find a happy place—sooner rather than later? Maybe the suggestion made you more anxious because when you let your mind soar anywhere it would like to go, it took you . . . nowhere.

No worries. We have a very enjoyable mission today. This is not about denial or putting one's head in the sand when life gets difficult . . . unless your happy place is indeed beneath the surface of a pristine beach. A happy place is a setting that brings joy to your spirit when you envision it. Thinking on beauty during harder times reminds us that difficulties pass and God's presence remains.

Sit back. Relax. Now think through settings and locations you've been. Walk me through places the kid version of you may have explored. Many people have a fond memory of a special tree. One that served as a personal jungle gym or housed a leaf-shrouded fort and lookout tower. Your senses can lead you. Spend a few moments reflecting on the scents, sounds, tastes, or physical sensations which mentally transport you to a place.

Let's keep going. What is the best vacation you've ever had? Best trip? Savor the experience of scanning the scenes and see if your mind likes to land on one in which you are joyful, free, surprised by delight. Maybe in that instant you felt wholly authentic and not one ounce of you felt obligated to apologize for you being you or for wearing the wrong clothes or laughing louder than others.

Where have you longed to visit? If you've ever vowed, "Someday I will go to . . . ," pay attention to that. The destination you mentioned in high school geography class might be different from the location you stated emphatically years later the first time you earned vacation time, but perhaps they represent similar climates. Lush tropical greens, azure blue coastlines, small town main streets on fall days, fields of Tuscan sunflowers in the early warmth of spring.

When you look at photos and screensavers, I wonder what landscapes speak your love language. Wide-open spaces with sky and land dividing the view in equal, stunning measure. Narrow city streets with vendors sharing their goods and strangers nodding to you in the hustle. Unpopulated paths that meander beneath the forest canopy through shade and spotlights of sun.

Your happy place might be a familiar place. Your favorite chair in your home with wide arms to hold your mug and journal. The hill peak with a view of the pond in a neighborhood park. The pew at church where you prayed for a friend.

It might be the people who serve up the happy and not the location at all. I think of my grandmother in a floral apron standing at the head of the Thanksgiving table beaming with pride. The quirky study partners who met regularly at the campus coffee shop during my toughest college semester. A movie-loving friend sharing the fifth row from the front at the local indie theater.

You might experience deep peace when you imagine walking a stretch of a Mediterranean vineyard with Jesus. Your memories might transport you to stand beside a cousin on the edge of a lake dock, braced to push one another into the shocking, cool liquid.

Close your eyes. Focus on moments, people, and landscapes of peace that feed your spirit. You have so many happy places to choose from.

Thinking on beauty during hard times reminds us that difficulties pass and God's presence remains.

Care Package

Delivered to Your Heart

My special delivery to you today includes an inspiring guidebook to any location you fancy. A "Take me to my happy place" keychain to remind you that you have access to joy wherever you are. And lastly, I give you an album with a thousand photos of life moments so you can remember the people and settings that have shaped your capacity to experience happiness.

Explorations and Actions

Write or think about a setting that inspires you. What about it feeds your spirit?

_____

_____

_____

How could you make this moment, this place where you stand, your happy place for today?

_____

_____

_____

Your heart is your spiritual happy place where you commune with the divine. How would you describe the landscape of your heart? What is its texture, shape, design?

_____

_____

_____

How do you measure happiness? How does happiness physically manifest for you? Energy? Ideas? Calm bliss?

_____

_____

_____

God Sees Your Need

I have found that the places I identify as my happy places are those in which I encounter an abiding sense of God's presence.

> *When Jacob awoke from his sleep, he thought, "Surely the Lord is in this place, and I was not aware of it."*
>
> GENESIS 28:16

Self-Care Self Talk

Life is a gift. I can be aware of and tap into the joy of the Lord wherever I go.

I NEED...
an extra pair of hands

Here I am with my hands outstretched. I'm ready to take from you whatever you need help carrying, holding, or schlepping from the car to the house and back again. Your plate is full these days. I see heavy helpings of family responsibilities, stuff from every era of your life, and extra scoops of work. Did I miss anything?

Those arms of yours are stronger than others realize. Often you hold up others or you grip the anchor while people around you reach for your shirttails to stay steady in their own spot on earth. With stubbornness and faith you stay in one place while storms swirl about you.

In that same faith, you're ready to release some of this. Your arms are growing weary, your hands are cramping, and two of your fingers went numb about three years ago. Sit and take a breather while we figure out what you can take off the stack.

How about I take that scrapbook you started four years ago? I reach for a half-finished DIY project, a shopping list to buy new hardware for your kitchen drawers, and that batch of photos you wanted to scan to your computer. I know . . . you will get to those someday, but not today.

This is like a life version of the game Jenga! Something else tumbles into my hands. It's a velvet bag of . . . rocks? What? Oh, a load of guilt. Someone gave it to you and sold you a lie that it was a present that would make you strong. You do know that pretty packaging doesn't change the original intention or burden of the contents, right? B'bye. I toss it, and it lands with a satisfying thud in the trash can.

You're energized now. One of your numb fingers is moving! You're scanning the pile, eager to transfer something else to me. In a flurry, you pass off to me: that stack of recipes in case you go gluten free, passwords to online stores you visited when seeking the perfect outfit for your reunion, and a workout video in a format for a device you don't own anymore. Do you feel the burn of our progress?

Let me come alongside you as you head out into the world. While you drive, I can text your family and tell them about your progress today. What else can I do to help? You ask me to make changes to your online calendar. You're rearranging your plans to make room for unexpected wants of others. As we continue with the day, I notice you carry bags that are too heavy for you. Most of what is in those grocery and shopping bags is for other people. I reach to grab one, but you quickly say, "I got it!" and hurry to the car. After you have loaded and unloaded those, your hand remains in a gripped position. Unable to open. Unable to receive.

I admire your giving spirit. But I see your shoulders droop under the weight of all you carry physically and emotionally. While you were power shopping and ignoring my offer of help, I bought you your favorite iced drink. Sip on this and let me share what I've learned:

You are a natural at helping . . . and yet . . . receiving help is not your thing. Things won't change in just one day. We both agree on this. Yet, today you did ask for help. You knew you couldn't keep juggling at the rate you spin, toss, and deliver. This is a good start. You are closer to balance. To wholeness.

I admire your
giving spirit. But I see
your shoulders droop
under the weight of all
you carry physically
and emotionally.

Care Package

Delivered to Your Heart

The present I share with you today is a velvet bag that is *not* filled with the weight of guilt. It awaits notes to yourself about God's love or your prayers. A statue of open hands will inspire you to hold the world loosely.

Explorations and Actions

What do you need to move along or delegate today?

_____

_____

_____

In what ways do you help too much? What do you believe you risk losing if you say no to someone else and tend to your needs?

_____

_____

_____

What do you acquire? Are you surrounded by paper piles, half-finished projects, technology debris? List two steps you can take to lighten those accumulations.

_____

_____

_____

When you are overwhelmed, close your eyes. Imagine someone sitting beside you with open hands to receive the burden. How does this feel? Return to this image and the sensations of receiving help when you need it.

_____

_____

_____

God Sees Your Need

God has an open-door policy for you to come to him with your needs and for his love.

> The LORD must wait for you to come to him so he can show you his love and compassion. For the LORD is a faithful God. Blessed are those who wait for his help.
>
> ISAIAH 30:18 NLT

Self-Care Self Talk

Help is always available to me. I will notice what I need and give myself permission to lift that need to another and to God.

I NEED...
motivation

fancy myself a behavioral scientist today, and you are my study focus. I have my favorite notebook with me and am ready to explore what motivates you. First, let's establish your need. Complete this sentence: I need motivation to _____.
Second, let me say, *You can do this!*

Free yourself to draw from your strengths to press on with confidence and natural momentum. Determine your built-in mode of motivation and then apply it to your circumstance. Are you typically inspired before, during, or after completing an objective?

Before. You get excited dreaming about a project. Gathering research or mentally going through the possibilities builds interest and energy. Sharing about the desired, future positive outcome is a conversation you enjoy having. You're a visionary and idea-person. The joy you receive is intertwined with anticipation.

During. You like the dive-in phase. You're the one on a committee saying "can we just get started" because you like the motivation of next steps and committing. You ride the adrenaline of problem-solving and progressing once work is underway. You are a doer so even if some details get difficult, you're pulled along by creating and seeing progress. Once you're safely in this window of forward motion, you wonder what took you so long to get started. The day in and day out meaningful work gives you satisfaction.

After. You are motivated by a sense of accomplishment and seeing the end goal doing what it's intended to do. You get a rush out of checking things off the list and having something to show for the hard work. You like being able to say you've completed something. You try to extend the joy ride of delighting in a job well done, emphasis on done. The finish line is your bliss.

Chances are that you're currently longing for motivation in a phase that isn't your sweet spot. Here's the good news, you can translate the elements that fascinate you in your preferred phase into what you need for the phase you're stuck in. For example . . .

You are struggling with the During phase. Keep the dreaming spirit alive. If you're in the trenches of details and choices, focus on and have conversations about the impact this project will have. Speaking about future satisfaction will compel you. Invent how to do each step with your own flair and talent. Doing daily work doesn't have to squelch your creativity! Apply your entrepreneurial strengths at every juncture.

You are struggling with the After phase. Finishing can feel anticlimactic to you, so you might be tempted to delay completion. You need immediate tasks to feel alive and fruitful. Make honoring the completion of your project one of those immediate tasks. Celebrate. Tell others you've completed it and hit send so you don't procrastinate finishing. Instead, think on and write about what you've learned so your completed endeavor creates a teaching foundation for your next pursuit.

You are struggling with the Before phase. Starting something new makes you weary. However, motivation can be sparked. List your past accomplishments and have this handy as a reminder that beginnings lead to finished projects. Set incremental, attainable goals so you will have plenty of "mini-afters" to boost your energy through planning and then doing. Let yourself plan how you'll honor the finish line. This keeps your mind in the happy "after" phase as you map out something new.

You have what it takes to move forward. When you get stuck or frustrated, return to a mode that suits your ability and interest.

You have
what it takes
to move forward.

Care Package

Delivered to Your Heart

My imagined package to be dropped at your door includes a leather-bound notebook that has the pages you care about most—dream board pages for the Before phase, to-do lists for the During phase, and journal pages to reflect on the joy of completion for the After phase.

Explorations and Actions

Are you motivated by the before, during, or after stage of a project? Has this been true for you in past years?

_____

_____

_____

Which aspect of the process are you stuck in right now?

_____

_____

_____

Based on awareness of your motivation mode, what might you do to progress further today?

_____

_____

_____

_____

Has anything discouraged you and become a significant barrier to momentum or completion?

_____

_____

_____

_____

God Sees Your Need

Whenever you feel stalled in a task or a life season, no matter the phase, you can choose to partner with God for clarity, momentum, and guidance.

> *Jesus looked at them and said, "With man this is impossible, but with God all things are possible."*
>
> MATTHEW 19:26

Self-Care Self Talk

Joy and faith can infuse and compel every stage of my endeavors.

I NEED...
a soft place to land

When our paths cross during my morning walk, I notice a look of bewilderment in your eyes. Maybe even fear. You have a stack of pillows with you and something else. Is that bubble wrap? This is serious. I reach for two of the pillows and put them side-by-side on a bench so we can sit comfortably. I ask where you're going and you tell me that you have to make a pretty big leap and you're working up the nerve. You are about to embark on a change that you almost embraced years ago but backed out of because fear got the best of you. In those days, you made it as far as the launch point, saw the gulf you needed to get across, then turned around and scuttled back to your routine.

Occasionally we are gifted the time and patience to look before we leap. But often we are nudged by circumstances to jump the abyss that splays vast and uncertain between the way things used to be and the way of our new now. The transition you face will likely be a wonderful opportunity for personal awakening—that's the good news. But when you're midair over that chasm of change, and your suspended feet are eager for the solidity of a safe step, your greatest desire is for a soft landing.

When I was young, I loved the musky scent of fall leaves. A gathered pile was an open invitation to take a running tumble into them. It was exhilarating. When the crimson and ochre pile cushioned my moment of contact with the earth, it enveloped all of me: my faded jeans, my hand-me-down rubber boots, and my puffy red jacket. When I surfaced, I had a twig lodged in my ponytail and a bit of vertigo. Yet I knew to celebrate those inconveniences because they were desired evidences that I had soared.

You can claim that innate childlike joy and faith. The experiences that have caused you to become skeptical or scared need not define you more than your hope. If a lot of what-ifs are tripping you on your way to the leap, restore your balance and belief that God's gone before you to prepare for your landing. And if you made it safely to the other side and your mind spins with questions of what now, look for the open way ahead God has also planned.

The Wright brothers have nothing on you as you gain momentum to find a new job, trust the next step in a passion project, buy a home, move to a different state, rid yourself of a rut to make space for something new, or stand up for someone. Whatever is your personal leap, there will be a soft place for you to land. You might not come upon a large mound of leaves as you are catapulted through a career change, a relationship's trial, or the arc of an illness, but something better is planned. Close your eyes and imagine God's hands stretched out; divine fingers of support, community, help, encouragement, and prayer intertwined and poised to catch you.

You're in the middle of a trust fall.

God's mercy absorbs the weight of our heaviest human needs. Let it envelop all of you: your faded dreams, your hand-me-down worries, and your puffy red eyes. And when you surface and take a look at your new now, give yourself a moment to revel in victory—you might be disheveled and dizzy, but you, my friend, have soared.

The experiences
that have caused
you to become
skeptical or scared
need not define you
more than your hope.

Care Package

Delivered to Your Heart

The special delivery I wish for you today includes the softest, most lush pouf for you to fall into for a rest. Chamomile mint tea to ease your nerves after leaping. And a leather-bound edition of the book of Psalms to illuminate the refuge of God's presence.

Explorations and Actions

What transition are you facing, or what leap have you recently made? Was the moment of takeoff or landing the most difficult?

_____

_____

_____

When has God caught you, preserved you in the past?

_____

_____

_____

If you are close to the jump-off point, list your what-ifs. Then, next to each of those, write "God is with me."

_____

_____

_____

_____

_____

If you have landed and are frustrated about what to do next, list your "what now" worries. Next to each of those, write, "God has me here for a purpose and asks me to trust and listen."

_____

_____

God Sees Your Need

When we hurdle the chasm of change, whether toward progress or pain, we land in God's mercy and refuge.

> *Have mercy on me, my God, have mercy on me,*
> *for in you I take refuge. I will take refuge in the shadow*
> *of your wings until the disaster has passed.*
>
> PSALM 57:1

Self-Care Self Talk

The unknown I face with nervousness is a known God holds with certainty. I am not alone when I jump, soar, and land.

I NEED...
to feel all the feels

Let it out. You need to. You've been stuffing those feelings for a long time to keep things steady and sane. You thought you were successful until a few of those emotions escaped during an inopportune moment and used a megaphone to announce that you're actually not fine and are extremely upset about a recent loss, a parent's betrayal of your trust, a spouse's lack of empathy during a time you needed comfort, a friend's insensitive remark . . .

Sometimes the big reveal of all the feels happens over something silly, harmless. I got frustrated about whether to have a sweet potato or a yam with dinner. Do tubers usually ignite angst within me? Um, no. The side dish of emotion I served up to my family wasn't related to supper, it was related to stress at work and life overwhelm. So many feelings were brewing within me that singling out one seemed impossible. Getting irritated about dinner was evidence of my emotions' prison break.

You and I didn't intend to become adults who squelch the "pay attention!" cries from the soul. The distancing from the rumbles of emotions happens over the years because we want to . . .

be liked

be polite

present an image of having it together

press on during a loss that could sink us forever

not let someone else think they control us or
    our emotions

carry others' burdens and not make them
    feel bad about it

carry others' burdens and make them feel
    bad about it

stop feeling so we can stop hurting

make it through a day without crying or
    throwing objects

avoid following the thread of feeling to discover
    where a triggering emotion originated

This is the day for you to notice and release the emotions you have told to be quiet and invisible. This is a safe space. There are tissues to catch tears, foam baseball bats and padded boxing gloves for physical processing, pillows for gentle fights and for the naps needed after exhausting truth telling.

On the shelf is a journal for you in a cheery color. Record the times you asked your happiness to stay quiet when you feared your joy would insult someone's distress, your sense of accomplishment would magnify another's struggle, your light of possibility would spark unwanted remarks from the naysayers. Those times need to be brought to this safe space too.

This day is about freeing the feels to live openhearted. When we don't let ourselves feel anger, we miss the balm of peace. When we don't allow injustice to be known, we skip over the transformation of mercy and truth. When we tell happiness to sit down and quit cheering, we miss the blessings.

Ask the feelings to rise and be noticed, held, listened to, honored, and sent off with kindness and gratitude for speaking up. What makes its way to the open air first? Fear, excitement, regret, love, anxiety, anger, joy, sorrow? Lift each one and the story behind it to God's wisdom and compassion. Take your time. I'm right beside you. I have the boxing gloves on if you want to spar. I also would gladly play some soothing music that we can nap to. Whatever you need to let your feelings rise and be heard.

Ask the feelings
to rise and be noticed,
held, listened to, honored,
and sent off with
kindness and gratitude
for speaking up.

Care Package

Delivered to Your Heart

This gift bag includes one of those stress balls you can squeeze when anxiety increases. A punching bag for the rounds with bigger emotions. I've included a cashmere blanket to bring you comfort as you feel your feels.

Explorations and Actions

What feelings do you press beneath the surface lately? What do you think could happen if you let them up for air?

_____

_____

_____

_____

How have you kept emotions under control instead of noticing, expressing, or processing them? What mental trick or default do you use?

_____

_____

_____

Write a note to yourself or to someone else to request or give forgiveness.

_____

_____

_____

_____

What emotion echoes strongest from your past? Is it easy or hard to allow that emotion to be felt in your life today? Why?

_____

_____

_____

God Sees Your Need

Don't protect God from your pain. He sees the broken places and longs to offer healing and redemption.

> *The LORD is near to the brokenhearted and*
> *saves the crushed in spirit.*
>
> PSALM 34:18 ESV

Self-Care Self Talk

Honoring each emotion with grace and honesty will allow me to take in the gifts of healing.

I NEED...
a play date

Come out, come out, wherever you are. It's time to play. No, this isn't for the kiddos. It is for your creative spirit. We live with our noses to the grindstone and forget to look up with wonder. I feel bad for us, really. We're hardworking people. That's fine. We get a kick out of crossing things off a to-do list. Wait! When our only joys become task oriented, that is a teensy bit lame. Any human between the ages of three and thirteen would roll their eyes at our excuses:

I have too much work and too many responsibilities.
Later is a better time. I haven't skipped in years—I'll probably
trip. I used to be creative, but that was long ago. I didn't study
anything arty. I'm more of a crossword type . . . all those boxes
are comforting. I don't know how to play that game, where is
the rule manual? I don't have the play gene.

Let's reclaim our birthright to joy and cleverness. To make sure something seeps beneath our fear of looking silly and our mode of rigidity, here is a play list for you:

- Stand barefoot in the grass and then walk in a figure eight for five minutes. (We're starting easy, but this is actually a very freeing act to shift from doing to being and from producing to playing.)
- Skip up and down your hallway or in your driveway to get your recess mojo back. (I double dog dare you.)
- Get a sketch pad and pack of colored pencils, pens, or chalk. (You can put this task on your checklist and cross it off if that makes you giddy.) Spend an hour drawing and doodling so you get past the "I don't know what to draw" mope that usually means we're afraid our art will be judged.
- Create something with clay or playdough or mud. Build without judging the outcome.
- Paint a picture. Go with realism or impressionism. Use brushes or your fingers. Choose watercolors or those thick, cheap primary color sets you can grab at any drugstore. Just paint.

- Create an origami stork using tissue paper (or old to-do lists). Watch an online tutorial or wing it.
- Fold a piece of paper into quarters or eighths and cut out hearts, snowflakes, or paper dolls and tape them to your window for the neighbors to see evidence of your new proclivity for fun.
- Get a joke book and read through until you laugh for real. Sometimes corny is just what the soul needs.
- Choose a coloring book that sparks some creative inspiration. Color one page or more and put one up on your fridge so you remember this self-playdate.
- Invite friends over to play board games. Have a competition with teams or a marathon of several games in a row.
- Open a dictionary to a random page and choose a word. Now write a poem or a song chorus using that word.
- Find out if there is a roller-skating rink still in existence in your area. You know what to do.

Surely, there will be three of these you will free yourself to do. If your first thought was "Okay, Hope, but quit calling me Shirley," then my work (or play) here is done!

Let's reclaim
our birthright to
joy and cleverness.

Care Package

Delivered to Your Heart

The playdate care package includes an endless supply of craft paper and colored pens, a stack of movies you will find funny, and a permission slip to let your guard down and not care what others think.

Explorations and Actions

When is the last time you were playful? Why do you need more play in your life?

_____

_____

_____

_____

Which of the playdates described today will be your invitation to return to the art of play?

_____

_____

_____

_____

How do you feel when you play? Nervous, out of control, free, young, embarrassed, empowered?

_____

_____

Consider in what areas you need more pleasure, flexibility, and freedom to have joy and reduce your judgment and rigidity. How might you bring the spirit of play into those areas?

_____

_____

_____

God Sees Your Need

God's love is freeing, it invites you to rejoice. Reflect your Creator's delight with delight.

> _The LORD your God is with you, the Mighty Warrior who saves. He will take great delight in you; in his love he will no longer rebuke you, but will rejoice over you with singing._
>
> ZEPHANIAH 3:17

Self-Care Self Talk

Play is good for my body and soul and connects me to the full nature of God.

I NEED...
balance

ately you have felt lopsided. It's a strange word and an even weirder experience to walk through your days with the sense that something is off. There's too much of this and too little of that. And like the famous "who's on first?" routine, you become befuddled figuring out exactly what is *this* and what is *that*!

You press on because you're good at keeping life in motion and playing it like you're fine. Only those in your inner circle notice that you sigh before you speak, as though exhausted by any effort and that you get flustered when something is asked of you immediately—like a decision! It's time to restore balance:

Between Giving and Receiving

Determine which of these dominates. Are you giving greatly from self, time, resources, and energy and have forgotten how to receive assistance and generosity from others? Choose one task or need to ask for and get help with. You are likely overdue for an indulgence that will reboot your balance. Or plan today for a favorite form of pampering or inspiration.

If you're in a pattern of receiving, achieving, accumulating, or fixating on your life, then change gears and choose one way this week to focus on someone else's needs or their happy moments. Reach out to them and connect. Ask questions about their life and pray with them.

Between Noes and Yeses

I can tell when you would like to say no but feel too guilty to follow your gut. When someone asks for a commitment, you look down, to the extent your eyelids are nearly closed. It's as if you're giving yourself a mini-timeout. But instead of declining the commitment as every part of your being begs you to do, you open those lids and your phone calendar and say yes. Next time, be your best advocate. Say no and thank you. Don't add "but maybe later" unless you really mean it. We do this to assuage our guilt, but it hurts us and others later.

If you've encountered a discouraging series of noes, give yourself a yes. A tactic in sales is to get a few yeses out of someone so that when the big ask is presented, their mind is warmed up for agreement. If the big ta-da you long for is not happening, present yourself with two smaller yes steps. For example, someone placed a no-go label on a dream or project you have. That's their prerogative. You, however, can say yes (#1) to creating the project without an outcome secured. And you can say yes (#2) to seeking a kindred spirit who will hold your endeavor with honor while providing constructive help and encouragement.

Between Faith and Fear

I will not be advocating that you balance faith with a spirit of fear! However, most of us become off-kilter because we give power to fear instead of God in our choices, beliefs, relationships, pursuits, and even prayers. We ask God for guidance, meanwhile we ground ourselves with "get real" self-talk that undermines hope. Today, bring to God a request for a next step, change, sense of clarity, or an answer. Thank God in advance for responding and for holding the whole of your life in his loving hands. If a fear-laced "what if" appears, do one of two things . . . follow this worst-case scenario vine of thought and then give that whole made-up situation to God *with* faith that he'll be there shaping goodness in your life. Or give that what-if seedling to God and thank him for covering your fear and doubt with his peace.

Most of us become off-kilter because we give power to fear instead of God in our choices, beliefs, relationships, reactions, pursuits, and even prayers.

Care Package

Delivered to Your Heart

Self-care is so important to a balanced life. This gift is for pampering—a basket filled with soothing scents to calm your mind, bath salts to relieve body tension, and a moisturizing foot mask.

Explorations and Actions

Take a moment to examine what you feel are priorities and why. List the first few that come to mind.

_____

_____

_____

_____

Use an interactive planner to track the hours you worry will slip away and to set aside times to incorporate two well-being practices. Which two?

_____

_____

_____

_____

Write a prayer asking for faith over fear in a current situation.

_____

_____

_____

_____

_____

_____

Take a walk in a local garden or park to help you clear your thoughts and give you the much-needed head space to contemplate your next step toward healthier living.

God Sees Your Need

God is right here with you. Find the time in your day to pray and to seek equilibrium.

> *Do not be anxious about anything, but in every situation,*
> *by prayer and petition, with thanksgiving, present*
> *your requests to God.*
>
> PHILIPPIANS 4:6

Self-Care Self Talk

Balance is not elusive. I can make a commitment to honor myself, learn to say no, and seek God's help.

I NEED...
to honor life moments

Changes shape the moments of significance that deserve our attention. I don't know about you, but so often my survival-mode mind trumps my good intentions to be awake to my life. So I'm excited about honoring life moments together.

Ritual sounds so formal. But ceremonial rituals aren't just for holidays or rites of passage (though those are perfect opportunities). They are for creating holy days . . . and moments. They help us honor what matters. What needs to be seen. Felt. Acknowledged. Examined. Savored. Protected. Shared. Respected. Marked. Rituals invite a sense of the sacred to a life event.

Your life is chock-full of moments worthy of caring attention and honor. Reverently observe the experiences that shape you. Are you experiencing any of these?

An ending. Are you closing a chapter on a job? Dealing with the heartache of a broken relationship? If you are selling a home or making a move, this is a time of departure from the known. You might be saying good riddance to a season of inertia . . . a desert time when it seemed like nothing was happening, sprouting, taking shape, and you're delighted to turn your face toward the sun of what comes next. Endings deserve a pause to honor the effort and gifts the experience represents. Don't let them pass by without recognition.

A beginning. Maybe you just signed a book deal, adoption papers, a contract to build a new home, a new employee form for the position of your dreams. A baptism is already a ritual but is an important one to honor in a personal way. Your beginning might be more subtle. Perhaps you chose this month to commit to a new hobby, a healthy habit, a spiritual discipline. (Way to go!)

A milestone. Are you the parent of a child who is transitioning to adulthood? A ceremony to mark and bless this life season will empower them. Maybe you are finally retiring (hooray!). Or you've completed a degree program. Is this a special anniversary for your marriage or of the day you pursued your passion? Will this upcoming birthday be a significant one? For a milestone birthday, I planned a dream trip of a week in New Mexico followed immediately with a week in New York. I will forever savor the memories of honoring my life in two special landscapes.

Loss. The loss of a beloved family member, friend, or pet can shake our foundations. While this can be difficult to think on, the practice of creating a ritual is very healing. Even if you participated in a memorial service, consider a personal ritual as well to say goodbye, honor the one who passed, and embark on the grieving journey in your own way.

Here is a possible ritual flow to do just that:

- Choose a theme. This will guide your other choices.
- Begin by praising God as the Creator of life, beginnings, endings, and the moments in between.
- Light a candle or place an object on the table that suits this occasion. An element from creation can be meaningful, such as a flower, a shell, a stone, a feather.
- Read a poem or verse or write something original to read.
- Do something that suits the life event . . . go for a walk, sing a song, plant a flower, invite friends to honor the experience.
- Close with a prayer of gratitude.

This practice will help you appreciate the unfolding of your life and be grateful for the holy hands that shape you, embrace you, carry you.

Your life is chock-full
of moments worthy
of caring attention
and honor.

Care Package

Delivered to Your Heart

Open this gift basket and see what's here for you: a scrapbook to keep photos and mementos, a treasure box to keep items of meaning from your times of transition and growth, and a book of blessings to honor transitions and milestones.

Explorations and Actions

What experience do you wish you had paused to notice? Spend time journaling about your recollections of that time.

What milestone would you like to honor with a ceremony? Look at the short plan in today's offering and see which suggestions you'd like to try.

Being a witness to your life is a way to honor God. Pay close attention to and hold with reverence special conversations, small victories, breakthroughs, and joys.

Who in your life could use a ceremony to mark a change, decision, or season of significance? Host a small gathering or a time for the two of you to notice together a moment of meaning.

God Sees Your Need

Each dawn, God gifts you with opportunities to rejoice in the gift of life and all that he's brought you to and through. Honor these ongoing beginnings with joy.

> *This is the day that the LORD has made;*
> *let us rejoice and be glad in it.*
>
> PSALM 118:24 ESV

Self-Care Self Talk

I will notice and honor the beginnings, endings, milestones, and transitions that form my path.

I NEED...
to let go

You seem extra motivated today. There's a bit of a fire in your eyes. The day you needed an extra set of hands to get rid of stuff inspired you for today. You are ready to let go of the emotional and spiritual baggage. I admit that tossing away your velvet bag of guilt felt good, even to me. Count me in!

There's nothing better than releasing heart burdens into the wild. So let's head to nature. There's a huge rock on the west-side riverbank with a smooth top just perfect for perching and watching the flow below. As we follow the path, the sound of water rushing over stones and aged tree roots grows louder. I feel the lure to be away from the confines of a normal day, and you're eager too. Your pace quickens. We get to the rock in no time and maneuver the well-placed crags to climb to the top.

The birds are chirping, and I see a squirrel. That counts as "the wild" in my book. What do you want to release first? You gesture with your hands that there is so much inside of you. I round up some small rocks within reach and place them between us. I'll suggest some burdens to surrender. Then we can each cast a rock into the river to let it go.

"Anxiety over something you can't control." You toss the rock. I toss mine in right after.

"Unforgiveness of self." Plop. Plop.

"Small disappointments that have become a foundation for discontentment." Spiral throw.

"Unforgiveness of someone who hurt you." Look at the splash those rocks make.

"Resentment for a time when someone tried to make you feel small."

"Loss of a dream." Our rocks collide in the air and fall together into the current.

"Grief that you never processed." You nod and throw the rock with force.

We're almost out of rocks when you reach into your pocket and retrieve a worn, torn piece of paper. This is your next item up for bidding adieu. You pull away when I reach for it and the paper floats and lands writing-side up on the lower ledge of the rock. The one word is faded but clear: "Shame."

I look at you. You look at me. I don't know the circumstance, but I can tell by the creased corners you've carried it for years in many different pockets and moving boxes. Are you ready to get rid of this? Yes. I grab a pinecone and you wedge the paper between its scales.

Merciful Creator, please take this burden from my friend.
Give her peace that flows through the wounds caused
by shame. Please take from her whatever she needs to entrust
to your hands. Bless this time of release and healing.
Empty her of all that blocks her hope. Thank you for
the freedom found in your grace. Amen.

You toss the pinecone. The breeze catches it and lowers it gently to the water's surface. It bobs and dips below the rippled waves a few times. A baptism of sorts. We watch it rise again and float until out of view. It is then that we both let go of a big sigh . . . a sigh of gratitude.

There's nothing better than releasing heart burdens into the wild.

Care Package

Delivered to Your Heart

My gift for you today is a basket of stones to toss in the water at your next letting-go session. A fishing pole (surprise!) so you can practice the art of catch and release and apply that skill to your worries too. A pair of ten-pound dumbbells are for those times when you are in the mood to pick a burden back up.

Explorations and Actions

List three people, circumstances, or hurts you want to—*need* to—let go of.

Which of those three is the hardest to release and why do you think that is?

What do you look forward to doing, feeling, or being when you feel emotionally lighter?

_____

_____

_____

_____

Who do you need to forgive? Who do you want forgiveness from?

_____

_____

_____

God Sees Your Need

You don't have to be at the river's edge to turn over your hurts, needs, or difficulties to God. The offer is always there because God is always there.

> _Cast your cares on the Lord and he will sustain you;_
> _he will never let the righteous be shaken._
>
> PSALM 55:22

Self-Care Self Talk

Letting go of a burden is not giving in. When I release my hurts, I am freed to accept goodness and abundance.

I NEED...
to hear everything will be okay

Your heart is weary. Things are uncertain. Assurances seem false or not convincing. When you bring your worries to others, sometimes they take them over and add in their version of woe that drowns out your vulnerable sharing. Or they spin your concerns further away from certainty and you walk away with a bigger burden rather than one halved and shared.

Express the underlying worries you haven't been able to say aloud in your moments of solitude or in the company of others.

This is my circumstance:

_____

_____

This is my deepest worry:

_____

_____

I'm paying attention to each word as you say it and how you say it. I notice your body language: hands motioning to express endless tumbling of thoughts, head down in discouragement, clenched fists showing frustration that maybe you have reached an end of your faith when you need it most.

I lean in when you share the worry beneath the worry and how it is starting to control your days and thoughts. Not long ago, you would have made progress toward peace by shaking off a persistent question or distracting yourself from a worry with thoughts of what is good and true. You need a hope you can feel beneath your restless feet. You need a promise to hold in your palm like a coin of great value.

When I ask how this time is different, you say your spirit is reluctant to believe. It is self-protective. You've been let down before by people and at times you've felt let down by God when circumstances did not unfold the way you had hoped and prayed they would.

Everything is going to be okay.

I don't offer that glibly. Your source of hurt resides deep within and the worry pervades your every cell. What you face isn't easy. Hope does not dismiss the pain of your plight; it illuminates the character of your Creator. I will say it again so you can hear it throughout your physical and spiritual self: Everything is going to be okay.

God is meeting you in this present moment with a peace that surpasses all understanding. Your mind will want to make sense of it, but your spirit knows to receive this peace without questioning it, without doubting it. Let yourself breathe in without fear squelching your intake of oxygen and renewal. You are covered by the love of Jesus.

As you rest in this truth and the image of God's presence with you, you begin to see something that is not your current circumstance. It is the vision of God holding you and the changed situation in the future. You aren't following the what-if trail of the worry, you are standing solidly on the foundation of faith. A faith that speaks to you over and over that everything is okay in the hands and under the power of your loving Creator. You don't know what will happen. Only God knows this. You can know that you remain in his embrace through it all. There is not a minute when you're left alone. God's got you and the situation you were trying to manage in only your power.

Hope does not
dismiss the pain
of your plight;
it illuminates
the character of
your Creator.

Care Package

Delivered to Your Heart

The package for you includes a photo of you in the future when peace is evident in your smile and posture. There is a plate of cookies and a big glass of milk so you have simple comforts of childhood. I embroidered "Everything will be okay" on a pillow so you can rest in this belief.

Explorations and Actions

Which worry can you turn over to God's care right now? Which worry do you feel the need to hold on to longer and why?

_____

_____

_____

_____

_____

Draw a timeline of your life and note when you were discouraged or fearful about the unknown. Then note the times of resolution, understanding, and clarity. Reflect on how God has not left you behind.

Write a note to yourself from the future when you are on the other side of this current hardship.

_____

_____

_____

_____

_____

Go for a 15-minute walk outside and notice how beauty endures no matter what. Creation will refresh your spirit and your hope.

God Sees Your Need

You don't need to know what is around the bend. Allow yourself to lean into God's presence in this moment and in each moment to come. This can be your consistent practice of faith.

> *Do not be frightened, and do not be dismayed,*
> *for the LORD your God is with you wherever you go.*
>
> JOSHUA 1:9 ESV

Self-Care Self Talk

I am not alone in this. When belief is difficult, I am not less loved by God.

I NEED...
a road trip

L et's get out of here!"

When I suggest this, you hesitate because you planned to do some paperwork. And clean out your email inbox. I feign a yawn while you scroll through your to-do list.

I remind you that just last week you mentioned how much you wanted to hit the road and experience the momentum of movement. You nod and sigh, remembering that wish.

Think about where you might want to venture. Do you need mountain air, a bustling city park, a scenic back road your family used to visit? The bliss of getting away isn't about the destination—it's about enjoying the freedom to go. We can always see where the road and your mood lead us.

Perfect. Now I'll help you create your go bag. What do we need to pack? What should be on every road trip checklist?

Snacks. Sweet or savory? Which of these fall under your

must-have category: chocolate, red vines (unless Twizzlers is your thing, no judgment), tortilla chips, cheddar crackers with spray cheese, snack cakes with cream filling, a tub of tapioca pudding (okay, I just judged a little), a loaf of French bread (you're redeemed), graham crackers, honey roasted cashews, turkey jerky, dried apricots, carrot chips, donut holes, fruit leather, string cheese, cake pops. How about those little candy wax bottles that anyone only buys so they can mold the wax into fake teeth or lips to wear for the fun of it? Let's do that.

Comfy clothes. You can wear your pajamas if you want. I don't care. Or maybe you'll bring those sweats you've had since college that no longer have a drawstring. Then again, yoga pants or your comfy jeans are probably a better choice. Definitely grab that soft cotton T-shirt and the knit sweater. Fuzzy slippers? Sure. I'll sound motherly here, but maybe pack some out-and-about shoes too.

Adventure accessories. Whether this is for three hours or two days, it could be fun to have binoculars or a telescope. While I'm a bit more into stargazing than birdwatching, I am game for whatever sounds just right for you. Um, how about camping chairs? Will we want those?

"Stop it with all the details," you say and grab the hiking

poles from my hands. All you wanted was to get in the car and go. The snacks come. The rest stays. I look at you sheepishly. Sorry I took it over. I'm supposed to be helping you in this journey, not adding complications.

As we leave the neighborhood and make our way beyond the streets we know so well, we both smile. You roll down the window to wave goodbye to the storefronts and restaurants you drive by every day. We could do this any weekend, but we don't. However, today we are people who head out and move beyond roads we've memorized to see trees, hills, people, or bridges and structures that aren't a background to daily routine. You share about how this month feels like last month and the one before. Sometimes a simple shake-up, even for a day, is all it takes to clear the head and the grime of the daily grind.

I lower my window and gulp air the way dogs do when owners give them six inches of sky during an errand run. I laugh. This unplanned momentum is lovely and freeing. I'm glad this is what you needed. It's what I needed too. (Which you knew all along.)

The bliss of getting away isn't about the destination— it's about enjoying the freedom to go.

Care Package

Delivered to Your Heart

The go-bag I wish for you is filled with a trip diary so you will record and recall memories that transport you from fret to freedom. The special souvenir you wish you had chosen during a past adventure. And last of all, a personalized bumper sticker so you can proclaim your destination. What does yours say?

Explorations and Actions

What aspect of a road trip speaks to you most right now?

_____

_____

_____

_____

What holds you back from following the impulse to explore and let a day unfold?

_____

_____

_____

_____

Recall a time when you did or did not give yourself permission to experience a free, unplanned day. What happened and how did you feel? Did you have regrets?

_____

_____

_____

_____

Plan your own road trip solo or with a friend. Where will you go and what will be your hope for this adventure?

_____

_____

God Sees Your Need

When you are on a new road that satisfies your longings, God will provide the guidance and nudges.

> *The heart of man plans his way,*
> *but the LORD establishes his steps.*
>
> PROVERBS 16:9 ESV

Self-Care Self Talk

The new view I observe during an adventure will inspire my outlook for the daily journey.

I NEED...
my life to count

They say to count your blessings. Well, today I want to count you as a blessing. That's right. You with your quirks and flaws (by now I know the real you), and you with a faith and generosity that inspire others. Nothing is wasted when you ask God to shape each of your days.

Today is just one of your precious windows of time to be you in the world. I think it is a worthwhile investment of these 24 hours to look at 24 ways your life has meaning. To help you recognize how much your life counts, I've created this list below, which, when finished, actually reflects 300 individual ways your life has created and continues to create good ripples in the world around you.

You have value because God loves you. This list doesn't represent tasks to master in order to earn meaning, it represents how your valued life becomes a vessel for meaning and purpose to flow from God's heart to yours and from your heart to that of another.

Let's pause and be a witness to the experiences that form your journey and become offerings to God and to others. Be fearless, honest, and open. Take stock of your seen and unseen expressions of love. Go through each one and spend time reflecting on these ways you share, connect, give, and live.

Can you think of . . .

One time you finally believed your worth in God

Two ideas you had that solved problems

Three organizations you support by donating
    or volunteering

Four times you embraced your purpose
    with boldness

Five experiences of fellowship or conversation
    with people you didn't know well

Six relationships you've nurtured

Seven times you forgave others

Eight times God forgave you

Nine experiences when you stumbled,
    got up, and pressed on

Ten people who love you

Eleven people you love

Twelve ways you've helped others this year

Thirteen new things you've learned and
applied to life

Fourteen conversations during which you
carefully listened to another

Fifteen moments of stillness when you
paused to listen to God

Sixteen memories of fellowship or inspiration
that you savor

Seventeen examples of God using you to
show his love

Eighteen ways you encourage others

Nineteen moments you leaned into
God's strength

Twenty examples of compassion you've
extended to others

Twenty-one ways you've used your gifts, talents,
and advantages for good

Twenty-two people or circumstances you've
prayed for or are praying for

Twenty-three hopes you have for yourself
    and others
Twenty-four reasons you have been grateful

Whether you are resting, sharing, struggling, laughing, grieving, reflecting, healing, or awakening . . . your life counts in every moment.

Pause and be a witness to the experiences that form your journey and become offerings to God and to others.

Care Package

Delivered to Your Heart

Here is a bejeweled calculator to match your microphone from earlier. (You can exchange it for an abacus if you have skills I was unaware of.) Either way, I want you to be able to add up your blessings and your ways to bless others. The next gift is a watch in your favorite style to remind you that every moment counts and you count in every moment.

Exploration and Actions

How did you feel after reading through these and reflecting on the 24 ways your life counts?

_____

_____

_____

_____

Which of the 24 was the hardest to come up with?

_____

Which of the 24 was the easiest to come up with?

_____

Choose one of the 24 expressions of love to emphasize this week. Journal about the experience of intentionally being a vessel for meaning to flow.

_____

_____

_____

_____

_____

_____

_____

_____

God Sees Your Need

Valuing your days and your life as God does will fill you with wisdom and gratitude.

> *Teach us to number our days,*
> *that we may gain a heart of wisdom.*
>
> PSALM 90:12

Self-Care Self Talk

What I do with this day is up to me. Meaning and love will be multiplied when I lift this day up to God.

prayer for a hope and a future

My phone is off. I'm lighting a candle to place between us. I look forward to lifting you and your life up to God. Today's offering has my prayer for you followed by words for you to pray if they echo your longings. May we both draw nearer to the Creator.

Giver of Hope and a Future,

My friend is ready to hold on to hope with a greater sense of possibility and faith. It is the desire to be more fully herself as your child that compels her to seek you now in this time of prayer. Give her glimpses of the times in her past when your promises have carried her, held her, protected her, guided her, comforted her. Looking at the path that has led up to this moment avails reminders of your faithfulness and gives her a sure place to stand now.

A heart of faith can grow weary under the weight of the daily stresses and the burden of long-term uncertainties. Bless my friend with refreshment . . . a stream of strength that flows through every part of her being. In the times when darkness is prevalent, dispel it with the light of confidence that is ignited by your provision and purpose.

She leans into who you are to rest her mind and to ease the impulse to fix things in her own power. With an abiding peace, she reconnects with the purpose that was born with her, in her. Steady her when she chases plans that are not intended for her. Reveal to her the path for a new season. Instill in my friend the hope of a future so she sees your signature on all things and never fears the stretch ahead. Each turn gives insight into the miracles and meaning you have in the universe for your children. Amen.

A prayer for you to meditate on today:

Shepherd of my life,

Share with me all that I need to know and understand for this moment in time. Gather my worries in your hand so that I cannot reclaim them and try to turn them into my truth. I breathe a sigh of relief knowing you are the one who holds my future and my today. Keep me from striving in ways that use up my energy and hope and yet never serve your purpose for my life. I know that following your truth does not assure me days of ease, but a constant faith does assure me peace that is beyond anything offered by the world or of my own making.

God, your love has freed me many times and in many ways. When I have been motivated to reach for something that wasn't in line with my purpose, you pulled me back into your embrace. You whispered to my spirit to wait and to watch for the beauty you are shaping for me.

I used to wish for things and then look with squinted eyes at the hazy future trying to see those wishes realized. Now I settle into this moment without the need to know. I have faith in your goodness and my worth in you. Wishes don't anchor me, but my identity in you does. This won't change tomorrow or ten years from now. You have not placed on me or anyone the burden to have life figured out. You ask only that I remain open, hopeful, faithful, and tender to your will. I can do this with gratitude. Amen.

Instill in my friend
the hope of a future
so she sees your
signature on all things
and never fears the
stretch ahead.

Care Package

Delivered to Your Heart

My imagined gifts to you today include a silver dish and a set of tealight candles so you can start your personal prayer time with the light of hope. And an elegant daybook with welcoming blank pages so you can record your prayers and the dreams God gives you for your future.

Explorations and Actions

What hope do you sense stirring in your spirit now?

_____

_____

_____

_____

_____

_____

How has fear held you back from following a path of possibility?

_____

_____

_____

_____

_____

_____

Consider what you are trusting instead of God's faithfulness.

If you have trouble sleeping because concerns occupy your thoughts, return to today's prayers and read them right before bed.

Try a new way to pray. Consider doing a prayer walk, praying a Scripture passage, praying with a friend, or meditating on one aspect of God's character during a time of silence.

God Sees Your Need

God knows what is ahead. You only need to know *who* to follow.

> *"For I know the plans I have for you," declares the* LORD,
> *"plans to prosper you and not to harm you,*
> *plans to give you hope and a future."*
>
> JEREMIAH 29:11

Self-Care Self Talk

Nurturing my faith in this moment creates a place for me to stand with hope for my future.

WHAT I NEED
today...

Continue the practice of exploring your heart needs for the next two weeks and beyond. Write down the daily need, your hope, and your prayer.

My need today: _____

My hope: _____

_____

My prayer: _____

_____

_____

My need today: _____

My hope: _____

_____

My prayer: _____

_____

_____

My need today: _____

My hope: _____

_____

My prayer: _____

_____

_____

My need today: _____

My hope: _____

_____

My prayer: _____

_____

_____

My need today: _____

My hope: _____

_____

My prayer: _____

_____

_____

About the Author

Hope Lyda is a concept and content editor, writer, and spiritual director. For more than 20 years she has worked in publishing and comes alongside others to help them uncover their write direction. Hope's books, including the bestselling *One-Minute Prayers® for Women* and *Life as a Prayer*, have sold over one million copies and cover a variety of genres from fiction to prayer and encouragement.

Through the practices of writing and conversation, Hope helps others explore thoughts, ideas, experiences, and personal heart-messages. Whenever possible, she mixes humor and reflection to embrace spiritual wonder and connect in joy.

Her happiest days are those that include any combination of walking, journaling, talking life and faith, downing iced coffees, and catching movies at the independent theaters in her hometown of Eugene, Oregon.

Hope earned degrees in journalism and film from the University of Oregon. She more recently received her spiritual direction training through the Stillpoint program hosted at Ghost Ranch in New Mexico.

Follow Hope at **@mywritedirection** or visit her at **www.mywritedirection.com**.

More Inspirational Books by Hope Lyda
My Unedited Writing Life
One-Minute Prayers® for a Woman's Year
One-Minute Prayers® to Start Your Day
One-Minute Prayers® for Hope and Comfort
One-Minute Prayers® to Unwind a Worried Mind
One-Minute Prayers® for Women
One-Minute Prayers® for Young Women
Life as a Prayer
The Gift of Small Blessings
The Gift of Small Comforts
One-Minute Prayers® for Men (with Nick Harrison)
One-Minute Prayers® for Moms
One-Minute Prayers® for Wives
One Minute with Jesus for Women